Beyond Diversity

What the future of racial justice will require of U.S. churches

A Barna Report Produced in Partnership
with the Racial Justice and Unity Center
and with funding from the Lilly Endowment

Funding for this research was made possible by the generous support of the Lilly Endowment. Barna Group and researchers from the Racial Justice and Unity Center partnered in data collection, analysis and writing of the report.

RESEARCH & WRITING TEAM FOR *BEYOND DIVERSITY*:

Dr. Glenn Bracey, Assistant Professor of Sociology at Villanova University—Principal Investigator
Chad Brennan, Director of Renew Partnerships—Project Director
Daniel Copeland, Barna Director of Research—Research Design / Analysis, Interviewer
Dr. Michael O. Emerson, Sociology Professor & Department Head at the University of Illinois at Chicago—Principal Investigator
Brooke Hempell, Barna Senior Vice President of Research—Research Design / Analysis, Interviewer
Brittany Wade, Founder of Wildfire Research—Research Design / Analysis, Interviewer
Alyce Youngblood, Barna Vice President of Editorial—Editor

REVIEWERS:

David Bailey, CEO and Founder of Arrabon
Dr. Oneya Okuwobi, Sociologist, Author, Consultant

Contents

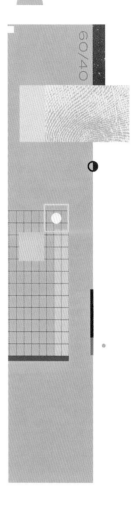

4   About the Research

6   At a Glance: Key Findings

9   A Welcome from Dr. Michael O. Emerson

13   Preface from Barna Group

19   Introduction by Dr. Glenn Bracey

22   Key Terms

25   1. Multi- & Mono-
       The realities of diversity in U.S. churches

43   2. Then & Now
       Acknowledgment of past and present racial injustice

61   3. "Me" & "We"
       Perspectives regarding systemic racism and individual prejudice

75   Splitting the Pews
       Exploring the gaps in views of race, in graphic detail

81   4. Privilege & Disadvantage
       Understanding how race impacts our lives

91   5. Us & Them
       How emotions and scripture factor into views of immigrants

103   6. Sunday & Every Day
       Opportunities to work toward solutions

121   Conclusion from Barna Group

       Appendix

131   A. Data Tables

137   B. Methodology

138   C. Acknowledgments

141   D. About the Project Partners

143   E. End Notes

About the Research

Dr. Glenn Bracey

PRINCIPAL INVESTIGATOR

Glenn Bracey, Ph.D., is an Assistant Professor of Sociology & Criminology at Villanova University and an expert on race and social movements and the law. He has also published research and regularly provides commentary on racism in evangelical churches.

Chad Brennan

PROJECT DIRECTOR

Chad Brennan is director of Renew Partnerships, a Christian non-profit organization that guides ministries and universities toward a biblical and effective approach to racial justice and unity with training and assessment resources. He previously served in campus ministry internationally with Cru.

Daniel Copeland

RESEARCH DESIGN / ANALYSIS, INTERVIEWER

Daniel Copeland serves as Barna Group's Director of Research. With a Masters in Sociology from Georgia State University, his work applies academic social research to Christian ministry and non-profits. Before Barna, he consulted local race and justice initiatives on research best practices.

Dr. Michael O. Emerson

PRINCIPAL INVESTIGATOR

Michael O. Emerson, Ph.D., is a Professor and Head in the Department of Sociology at the University of Illinois, Chicago. He has published 15 books on his studies of race, religion and urban sociology, including groundbreaking research in *Divided by Faith*. Dr. Emerson previously taught Sociology at North Park and Rice Universities.

Brooke Hempell

RESEARCH DESIGN / ANALYSIS, INTERVIEWER

As Senior Vice President for Barna, Brooke Hempell has directed Barna's published studies as well as strategic research for Christian ministry and non-profit clients for six years. Her focus includes issues of social justice, faith development and generational science. Prior to Barna, she conducted research and consulting for corporate clients in healthcare and financial services.

Brittany Wade

RESEARCH DESIGN / ANALYSIS, INTERVIEWER

Brittany Wade is the COO of UNDIVIDED and the Founder of Wildfire Research. With a background in commercial market research, including seven years with Nielsen, she now offers consulting, research and data analysis to ministries and non-profits. She previously was on staff with one of the country's largest churches, developing research and programming to serve their constituents.

How We Did This Study

The research team desired a multidisciplinary, multifaceted methodology to investigate racial dynamics in the U.S. and in the Church. We approached this complex topic through multiple dimensions with the hope of producing robust, actionable and representative insights and building upon past research and literature. We invited academics, thought leaders and local leaders to join a collaborative team to provide crucial input and review along the way. Our qualitative research phases included interviews with experts, church leaders and church staff, and focus groups with congregants in multiple cities and churches. Our quantitative research was conducted online with a robust, representative sample. We consulted with multiple reviewers, both experts and laypeople, to ensure thorough, credible and accessible data reporting.

Our Research, by the Numbers

68 Collaboration Team Members

These leaders generously dedicated their expertise and time to providing project direction, reviewing the research design (including the quantitative survey instrument and discussion guide) and reviewing research results.

119 Interviews with Experts & Leaders in 10 Cities

To ensure this research was informed by past research and leading-edge work being done around the U.S., these leaders gave time to meet with the research team and provide their insights. Their thoughts informed the research design.

35 Interviews with Church Staff

These interviews detailed the hardships, successes and failures faced in three churches that are intentionally pursuing racial unity, reconciliation and justice.

2,889 U.S. Adults & Practicing Christians Interviewed in a Representative Survey

The survey over-sampled practicing Christians and Black, Asian and Hispanic adults, and was representative by age, gender, race / ethnicity, region, education and income. Each of the 65 questions was intentionally designed to either connect to past research or investigate new hypotheses.

32 Focus Groups with 200 Congregants from 20 Churches & Five Cities

At both racially diverse and homogeneous churches, focus groups with congregants and facilitators of the same race and gender were interviewed about their experiences and perspectives of justice, their churches and the U.S. ◼

At a Glance

Diverse congregations are perceived as an answer to racial injustice

80 percent of practicing Christians say the Church can improve race dynamics in the U.S. by welcoming people of all ethnicities.

Diversity can sometimes inflict more harm than good, especially where Black worshippers are concerned.

29 percent of Black practicing Christians in multiracial congregations, compared to 11 percent in monoracial Black congregations, say they have experienced racial prejudice in church.

Many Christians are not moving toward progress on racial justice.

From 2019 to 2020, after the racial reckoning that occurred in the summer of 2020, the proportion of practicing Christians who are unmotivated to address racial injustice increased by 13 percentage points.

Many white practicing Christians are reluctant to acknowledge systemic racial injustice, despite reports from their Black peers in the Church.

Three in five white practicing Christians say personal prejudice is a bigger problem than discrimination built into institutions; two-thirds of Black practicing Christians say institutional discrimination is a bigger problem than personal prejudice.

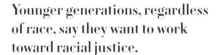

Younger generations, regardless of race, say they want to work toward racial justice.

The majority of Christian Millennials and Gen Z is aware of and motivated to address racial injustice. Younger generations are still in need of an education, though, as they are no more likely than other generations to actually identify specific forms of systemic discrimination.

Our research shows that a large percentage of Christians of color has a rich, personal understanding of the Bible's teachings on justice and concern for the oppressed.

Generally, practicing Christians of color outpace white practicing Christians in applying biblical passages regarding caring for the vulnerable and marginalized.

Churches where people of color have significant representation and shared influence show healthier patterns in relationships and views on race.

When a practicing Christian's identity is reflected in the racial composition of the leadership team, they face fewer hurdles in their worship community.

See "Splitting the Pews" on page 75 for a visual summary of some of the starkest and most poignant divides observed in our research.

from Dr. Michael O. Emerson,

RACE, RELIGION & JUSTICE PROJECT
PRINCIPAL INVESTIGATOR

A Welcome

Racial Injustice: A Stubborn Disease

In 2000, my colleague Christian Smith and I published *Divided by Faith: Evangelical Religion and the Problem of Race in America.* It helped to start a wave of interest in forming multiracial churches, as well as accompanying networks, organizations, books, conferences, training programs, papers and more. Those efforts have produced demographic change in many churches. Since 1998, the percentage of demographically defined multiracial churches (using the previous statistical standard, defined as no one racial group making up 80% or more; see Key Terms on page 22 for a revised standard) has grown from 6 percent to 16 percent, nearly tripling in two decades. And among Protestants, the growth has been even more dramatic. For Mainline Protestants over the 1998 to 2019 period, the percentage of multiracial churches has grown from 1 percent to 11 percent. For evangelical Protestants, from 7 percent to 23 percent.[1]

Despite all these efforts and the demographic successes, we still have a long way to go. In some ways, on some measures, things are even worse than they were 20 years ago. How is that possible? This report attempts to provide some answers to that question.

Racial diversity of churches was never to be the end goal; biblical racial justice, reconciliation and authentic unity are the end goals. Racial diversity was and is a biblical path to these (or, as some see it, one outcome of these). Because our end goals are our biblical calling, if we find barriers to them, we must in good faith identify the barriers and work to overcome them. We don't throw the proverbial baby out with the bathwater. We know our calling, and we work toward it. This is a lifecycle. As toddlers, we make mistakes and wobble, but healthy maturity means we learn from our mistakes and change for the better.

Racial injustice is like a disease. Our research has found that the disease has not gone away even as the supposed antibodies of multiracial churches have multiplied. Racial injustice has mutated into new forms, and it has proven highly resistant to the antibodies of multiracial church. This report describes the symptoms and the recommended treatments.

"Racial diversity of churches was never to be the end goal; biblical racial justice, reconciliation and authentic unity are the end goals."

Why is it so important for us to deal with this disease?

- In a recent Barna report, "divisions in the church" ranked shockingly low among a list of major concerns (selected by only 12 percent of pastors).[2] I am dumbfounded. Either we mistakenly believe there are no divisions in the Church, or we don't think them important. Any division in a church means the church is ill. If we are ill, our attention must be on healing. And to heal, we must understand both the symptoms and the treatment. If we don't, the Christian Church in North America will continue to fade.

- God will not forever stand idly by waiting for us to overcome division and injustice. We have been given the power of the Holy Spirit to do what the world cannot do. If we won't use it, we will lose it. And God will judge us. Our scriptures clearly tell us so.

What to Do if You Get Stuck

by Chad Brennan
DIRECTOR OF RENEW PARTNERSHIPS

This Barna report highlights a few key findings from our joint research that we hope will be helpful for Christian leaders who desire to make progress.

It is easy to get stuck in the complexities and challenges. Here are some recommendations in case you find the information in the following chapters a bit confusing and overwhelming:

1. **Remember that every step is likely to help:** Even if we don't get it "perfect," every step of progress can align us closer to God's will and lead to greater joy, health, peace and unity in our lives, relationships and organizations.
2. **Rely on the Holy Spirit:** Reflect on how the Holy Spirit has empowered Christians to overcome injustice and division for thousands of years. History shows us that what is impossible for humanity is no problem for the Holy Spirit.
3. **Pursue the support and help of a Christian community:** Participating in a workshop,

- As our nation and our world shake under the weight of inequality and injustice, the Church's time is now. Later will be too late.

What we have learned about treating the disease:

- Demographically defined multiracial congregations can make things better or worse. We will explore why.

- Though I am a strong advocate of multiracial congregations as a biblical model, given our times, homogeneous congregations led by people of color can serve as a safe haven for people of color and be strong voices for justice. But they too can make things better or worse.

- We must shift from racial diversity to racial justice and, eventually, reconciliation and authentic unity. Diversity on its own offers a bit of initial false hope but can actually lead to more harm than good in combatting the problem.

Our hope and prayer with *Beyond Diversity* is that it will help the Body of Christ more effectively work toward racial justice and authentic reconciliation and unity, our God-designed Christian witness.

attending a conference or reading a report like this typically isn't enough to bring about change. A community of Christians who are committed to racial justice and unity can provide the encouragement and help you need to make progress over the long haul.

4. **Pursue the support and help of experts:** In this report, we have the opportunity to learn from some of the leading experts in the country. That's great. But it is even more helpful if an expert can come alongside our efforts and walk with us through the challenges.

Prayerfully pursue an ongoing relationship with an experienced expert who can help you understand the content in this report and apply it in your life and organization.

Preface from Barna Group

This extensive report, funded generously by the Lilly Endowment, is the product of a unique partnership with our colleagues at the Racial Justice and Unity Center. This project includes findings from, to our understanding, the largest study of racial dynamics in U.S. Christianity to date. It's been Barna's honor to contribute to this crucial research effort over the past couple years. All the while, we've kept our focus on Barna's primary mission: supporting pastors and church leaders as they navigate change.

And on this subject of racial justice, we know Christian leaders will need massive support.

Nearly two-thirds of practicing Christians (64%) and 44 percent of the general population of all U.S. adults believe churches have a major role to play in improving race relations. Practicing Christians tell us they are both already listening to religious leaders *and* hoping to see them step up more in this area.[3]

First, the work our teams have done on race and the Church over the last three years leads us to believe the following questions are essential for leaders:

How am I stewarding the trust people have placed in me to lead on issues of race?

What incorrect attitudes remain unchallenged in my personal life and in my church or ministry that hinder biblical justice and unity?

What pain around racial issues in my own congregation or community have I remained unaware or dismissive of?

For better or for worse, how is the Church's reputation affected by my own ability to responsibly address and work toward racial justice?

How can the Church contribute to creating systems of racial justice rather than inequity?

Moving Beyond Diversity

In recent decades, there has been an increasingly popular assumption in the Church that racial equality and unity are best realized through—or perhaps could even be wholly accomplished by—cultivating racially diverse environments. A captivating vision for multiracial worship has taken root in many denominations. As researchers and conveners, we've heard from survey respondents, expert contributors and faith leaders around the country: *Diversity is the goal, the future.*[4] Our own research suggests this is of great importance to increasingly diverse younger generations and that exposure to and relationship with people who are different from you can help change minds and spark empathy.[5]

But statistical diversity, or mere physical integration, is not a panacea. Simply being in proximity to people of different racial backgrounds does not eliminate racism, nor does it always produce the positive outcomes that may be desired in bringing racial groups together for corporate worship. In fact, the pursuit of maintaining statistical diversity may directly prompt leaders to neglect racial justice.[6]

We believe the data highlight the need for a conversation focused on more than diversity. We want to help church leaders *in any context* navigate issues of race with clarity.

The goal of this report is not to make a case for either multiracial or monoracial worship. As you'll see, the research points to pros and cons in both types of churches. Rather, we believe the data highlight the need for a conversation focused on more than diversity.

We want to help Christian leaders *in any context* navigate issues of race with clarity. Even if a church body is completely racially homogeneous and has little chance of diversifying in the near future, its leadership can and should be equipping congregants to engage faithfully with matters of racial justice. Even a church body experiencing integrated worship may have challenges still to overcome; diversity is not an ideal to pursue blithely. Through these chapters, we'll uncover pitfalls and equip leaders to better understand views of and needs for justice and unity, and along the way we'll also point out traits of healthy diversity.

A New Lens

Each person brings their own level of race-consciousness into these discussions, affecting the way they see themselves and move through the world. Persons negatively affected by racial dynamics tend to think about race more often. Conversely, those who are advantaged by race rarely find occasion to reflect on race.

The lenses through which you might never look may be the ones your neighbor is always compelled to wear

Consider this: More than half of Black practicing Christians have their race in mind frequently, with nearly one-third (31%) saying this is "very often" the case. Their Hispanic peers follow in race-consciousness (21% "very often," 19% "often"). Asians are the minority population least likely to say they are often thinking about their race (13% "very often," 24% "often"). For white practicing Christians, however, their racial identity isn't much of a focus; six in 10 say their white identity is "rarely" (41%) or "never" (20%) on their mind.

In short, the lenses through which you might never look may be the ones your neighbor is always compelled to wear.

Recognizing Our Perspective

Here is the perspective we have brought to the creation of this report:

We are a research firm, with a predominantly white team, that has spent decades studying a segment of the Church where, presently, white Christians are the majority, and the bulk of pastors are white men over age 54.[7] We have taken great care to listen to and represent churchgoers, leaders and practitioners of color through quantitative and qualitative research as well as expert interviews—and indeed believe their voices, experiences and leadership are crucial on the path to racial justice and unity. This listening is a step in our own repentance toward segments of the Church we haven't fully represented and served in our work. This is a deficit our team intends to correct.

We have seen firsthand—both through the data itself and through the experiences of interpreting, writing about and sharing it—that no two people seem to understand and speak of race and justice in exactly the same way. Across generational, denominational, ideological and especially racial lines, the chasm grows. As we continue on this journey, you may find that, in this volume, some of the reporting and recommendations seem to hold a white Christian reader's understanding in mind. While we recognize that this is not a comprehensive report on the subject of racial justice and the Church, we are hopeful for the impact this research might have on several fronts.

First, we pray that the group who has been our primary audience—a group who may rarely think about even their own race in the day-to-day—will collectively rise to the challenge of learning about and supporting racial justice, listening to leaders of color and moving beyond diversity to deep expressions of the Body of Christ.

Second, we hope to build trust with leaders of color by engaging thoughtfully in issues that they have championed for many, many years. We see and acknowledge your good work and are eager to learn from and celebrate your leadership.

An important outcome for anyone reading this, and the other resources coming out of the study (see sidebar), is not just to understand or do but to be transformed: to see things you might not have before, to train yourself to listen and learn from other perspectives—something research gives us great power to do—to yearn for and be a part of deep, lasting, Spirit-driven change.

This is hard work, and we have been attempting it ourselves. We have been challenged by this project—as researchers, as co-workers and as members of the Church. As we have studied, we have also lamented. Even while the team has been organizing these findings into a manuscript, the U.S. has borne witness to another historic uprising for racial

Getting the Most from This Study

The following additional resources produced by the researchers can help you understand and apply the content in this book and make progress in racial dynamics in your life and organization.

BOOKS

- *Faithful Antiracism* by Chad Brennan and Dr. Christina Edmondson (Intervarsity Press, December 2021)
- *Ghosts in the Room* by Dr. Glenn Bracey (Expected fall 2022)

- *The Grand Betrayal* by Dr. Michael O. Emerson and Dr. Glenn Bracey (Expected fall 2022)

THE RACIAL JUSTICE AND UNITY CENTER

The Racial Justice and Unity Center, a new ministry of Renew Partnerships, was launched in 2021 and provides:

- **Research-based assessments**
  Individual and organizational tools based on national research and the input of leading experts

justice and the election of a woman of Black and Asian descent to the office of vice president. While the conversation has evolved—and become even more polarized in the nation and the Church—we've labored over the language and conclusions in this report, hoping they would be accessible, knowing they could be challenging and praying they might be impactful.

Encouragingly, we find ourselves able to share data that not only convict, but also instruct. Specifically, this research provides powerful examples of how empathy, empowerment of leaders of color and careful application of scripture might draw us closer to our neighbors and to a biblical vision of racial justice.

As Barna president David Kinnaman shared on our blog in June 2020, "There's no doubt this will be a lengthy and demanding journey, one that will call us all to continuous repentance, reflection and response. But we are up to the challenge and hope to encourage other followers of Christ to commit to the same journey."[8] ▓

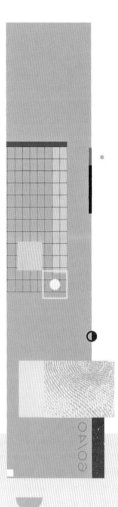

Coaching network
Ongoing mentoring and encouragement from experienced, knowledgeable coaches

Customized help for organizations
Guidance for churches, denominations, colleges, K–12 schools and ministries who want to design assessments, analysis and strategies for making progress

Please visit rjuc.org for details.

BARNA ACCESS PLUS

Get additional resources, webinars and related Barna research through the Race and the Church Channel. Learn more and subscribe at barna.com/raceandthechurch. ▓

by Dr. Glenn Bracey,
RACE, RELIGION & JUSTICE PROJECT
PRINCIPAL INVESTIGATOR

Introduction

A Vision for the Church Body

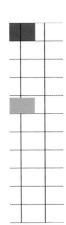

Occasionally, God invites me to reflect on the sheer beauty of his design and creation. He reminds me that his Church is beautiful, as every bride is to her groom. The vision of the Church is a gorgeous one, in which everyone is distinct yet moving in harmony. It is a singular body, made of many parts, that displays the glorious complexity and flawlessness of our God.

As our creator, God had the right to make us separate and unequal (Romans 9:21), but he instead chose to make us one, inseparable body (Romans 12:4–8). As one body, we are all equal in Christ, each with their individual function. Each moving seamlessly from moments of prominence to moments of seclusion. Each celebrating the other as we share in God's glory. That is the vision of the Church that we work to realize.

As researchers and authors, our goal for this report is to help the Church be the beautiful bride she is destined to be. We want to invite every Christian into the blessed community that is the Church, and we want to ensure that each member can bring and manifest the unique gifts God gave them. To realize God's glorious vision, we have to first examine where we fall short of it. *Beyond Diversity* spends much time revealing those shortcomings.

As you read, please remember that the aim of this report is to uplift the Church—not to shame it. We are like bridesmaids, working to ensure the bride is as beautiful and glowing as she can possibly be for her groom.

Trends in Responses of People of Color

At the moment, there is still much work to do. The Church is not living up to God's vision because it is not operating as the united body he designed. Much of this report is a discussion of divisions and ongoing struggles within the Church. As you will see in the pages that follow, there are many race-based points of division within the body of Christ. Indeed, we often find that those outside the Church are more unified on issues of race than are those in the Church. There are racial disagreements on nearly every question. The Church is divided about the character and significance of racial history, the realities and effects of contemporary racial discrimination and how and in what forms the Church should work to address inequalities, among many other issues. In short, we are divided by race.

"To realize God's glorious vision, we have to first examine where we fall short of it."

Our data reveal that racial divisions within the Church are not randomly distributed. Instead, there is a pattern in which the powerful and advantaged deny or minimize the social structures that sustain their dominance. For example, white adults are less likely than nonwhite adults to acknowledge the historical oppression of people of color in the U.S. Instead, they attribute racial disparities to nonwhites' deviant cultures and poor decision-making, whereas people of color attribute these inequalities to historical and contemporary discrimination.

That is not to say that people of color agree on all measures. Instead, there is a pattern in which Asians are more likely to give answers similar to white adults' responses, while Hispanic / Latino sentiments hover between those of white and Black respondents. According to our interviews with several scholars, this pattern may reflect Asians' and Hispanics' aspirations to have the same advantages as white Americans and a desire to avoid the negative stereotypes attached to Black people. As non-Black people of color, they may find themselves in an awkward position. On one hand, they need to account for the structural racism they face that is similar to the Black experience. On the other hand, they may perceive a need to distinguish themselves from African Americans, in part by denying the full impact of structural racism. Because they are wealthier and stereotyped as the "model minority," Asians may have more incentive than Hispanic and Black people to minimize the importance of systemic racism.

In any case, it appears that racial divisions and stereotypes in society are not only present, but often more concentrated, in the Church. As in the larger society, these racial divisions relate to current access to and hopes for power.

Equality & Interdependence

Jesus and the Bible's authors warned repeatedly about the threat that a desire for power is to the Church. Jesus chastises disciples who sought power over others (Mark 10:35–45) and instead teaches that Christians are not to be like Gentiles, whose great men exercise authority over others. Christians are to serve rather than dominate one another. And Christian equality and interdependence are to be irrespective of race or ethnicity, for in Christ, there is neither Jew nor Greek (Galatians 3:28). Then we will be the well-constructed temple (Ephesians 2:19–22), the unified body (Romans 12) that God describes.

The only way to be the united, egalitarian Church that God called us to be is to regularly examine ourselves to be sure we are living up to his vision. This report is just such an evaluation. Although we are currently falling short, there is still hope that we might put aside divisive interests in favor of the unity that Christ said would be the hallmark of his Church. ▨

Key Terms

Practicing Christians are self-identified Christians who say their faith is very important in their lives and have attended a worship service within the past month.

Gen Z were born 1999 to 2015.
Millennials were born 1984 to 1998.
Gen X were born 1965 to 1983.
Boomers were born 1946 to 1964.
Elders were born before 1946.

Due to smaller sample sizes, Barna cannot always report on Gen Z and Elders.

Multiracial & monoracial churches: As a statistical standard for this study, we refer to multiracial churches as those where no single racial or ethnic group comprises more than 60 percent of the congregation, according to practicing Christians' estimations of the congregational makeup. Monoracial churches, inversely, are those in which more than 60 percent of the congregation is racially or ethnically homogeneous.[9]

A Note on "Race" & "Ethnicity"

For the purposes of data collection and reporting, Barna categorizes respondents' racial and ethnic identities according to their self-descriptions (i.e., what respondents select from a list of demographic, survey-based options).

Also, as is standard in social research, random survey respondents were not given any definitions of race or ethnicity to react to; they simply answered questions based upon their own interpretation of those terms.

For the benefit of readers of this report, the project team offers the following definitions for race, ethnicity, culture and nationality. Though they are often used interchangeably and their definitions inform one another, there are important distinctions in their origins and meanings. Again, these definitions were not used in survey language, but are important in understanding the reporting of the study's findings, themes and applications. **Nationality** describes one's legal status of citizenship or belonging to a particular nation. **Ethnicity** is based on perceived cultural similarities which are often linked to a shared ancestral background or heritage. This may include one's nationality, but also may be defined by or exist in combination with one's language, religion, tribe or place of origin. **Race** is a set of socially created categories based on selected perceived differences in physical traits such as skin tone, facial features, hair texture, etc. **Culture** consists of beliefs, behaviors, objects and other characteristics common to members of a particular group.

What is meant by "systemic racism"?

Our project partners Drs. Glenn Bracey and Michael O. Emerson provide this additional context: This report strives to use the term "race" when the categorization of people groups relates to societal stratification or power.[10] Examples of how societal power is inequitably distributed by race can be thought of as **systemic racism** (or structural racism), which we'll first cover in this report in chapter three. What do we mean by this term? We define it as *institutionalized patterns that move material and symbolic resources from subordinate groups to dominant groups.* An example: The pattern of funding schools based on neighborhood wealth, knowing that neighborhoods are racially segregated and that white neighborhoods are wealthier than neighborhoods where people of color live, guarantees that white Americans have better education opportunities than other people. White neighborhoods are wealthier than neighborhoods where people of color live because, among other reasons, in the first half of the 20th Century, the U.S. government explicitly provided better neighborhoods to white families (through means such as redlining or legal restrictive homeowner covenants). ■

1. Multi- & Mono-:

The realities of diversity in U.S. churches

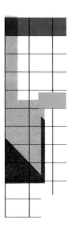

The title of this report indicates that diversity is not the destination of the Church's role in racial justice, and in this chapter we'll examine an early and important signpost: Some of the Church's best efforts toward unity in recent decades seem to be insufficient in helping to understand or rectify the challenges experienced by worshippers of color, especially Black individuals, for whom issues of race in the U.S. are front and center.

Let's compare two types of churches a Christian of color might attend.

One has been touted as a small glimpse of scripture's image of heaven, as a crowd comprising "every nation and tribe and people and language" (Revelation 7:9). It's what is now commonly described as a multiracial church, a model many today seek to emulate. Like the early Church in Acts, it's a diverse representation of many cultures. Specifically, per the definitions for this study, let's say it includes no more than 60 percent of a single racial or ethnic group.

The other type of church is more homogeneous than this statistical standard, veering toward monoracial.

In one congregation, this attendee of color is more likely to experience racial prejudice or even sense pressure to forfeit markers of their racial identity. Relationally, they may struggle to connect with others or to move into leadership positions.

According to our research, prejudice still exists and is more often experienced in diverse churches than in those that are monoracial.

Perhaps you'd assume that a congregation that succeeds in drawing attendees of multiple races would be truly welcoming. The challenges depicted in these charts, however, are profound: Almost three in 10 Black practicing Christians in a multiracial church (29%) say they have experienced racial

. . . Which worship environment would you assume is multiracial?

▦ Black practicing Christians in multiracial churches
■ Black practicing Christians in monoracial churches

"I have experienced racial prejudice in my church"

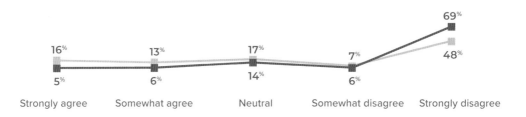

	Strongly agree	Somewhat agree	Neutral	Somewhat disagree	Strongly disagree
Multiracial	16%	13%	17%	7%	48%
Monoracial	5%	6%	14%	6%	69%

"I feel pressure to give up part of my racial / ethnic identity in my church"

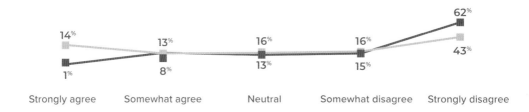

	Strongly agree	Somewhat agree	Neutral	Somewhat disagree	Strongly disagree
Multiracial	14%	13%	16%	16%	43%
Monoracial	1%	8%	13%	15%	62%

prejudice on some level. Granted, racial prejudice may still exist in the monoracial environment; even predominantly Black churches, on average, have a small percentage of non-Black worshippers, and in some cases colorism (prejudice based on skin tone within the same ethnic or racial group) could also be occurring. Even so, just 11 percent of Black practicing Christians report facing prejudice in a monoracial Black church. There is

▦ Black practicing Christians in multiracial churches
▦ Black practicing Christians in monoracial churches

"I find it difficult to build relationships in my church"

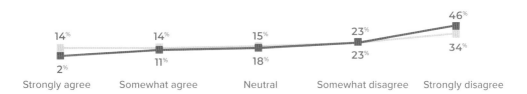

14%	14%	15%	23%	46%
2%	11%	18%	23%	34%
Strongly agree	Somewhat agree	Neutral	Somewhat disagree	Strongly disagree

"I find it difficult to move into leadership positions in my church"

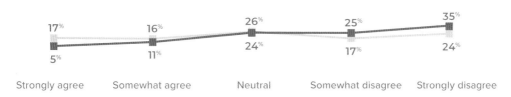

17%	16%	26%	25%	35%
5%	11%	24%	17%	24%
Strongly agree	Somewhat agree	Neutral	Somewhat disagree	Strongly disagree

n=258 Black practicing Christians, July 19–August 5, 2019.

potentially greater cost for the Black worshipper who moves into a more diverse congregation and begins to have more cross-racial interactions in that faith community.

More than one-quarter of Black practicing Christians feels pressured to give up part of their racial or ethnic identity in a multiracial church (27%) and finds it difficult to build relationships there (28%). Finally, one-third of

In Focus: Assimilation in Multiracial Churches

"Sometimes *multiethnic* means the culture's still white. You say you're multiethnic, but the leadership is white, and the music is white, and the power structure is still white. So, there's really no dynamic change there." —*Black congregant*

"When I participate in other things, if it is a women's camp or if it is small groups, the perspective and the lens that is spoken about is a white lens. I can give a specific example of participating in a small group and asking about strongholds and about race and being told that we are to love everybody. Yea, they want Black people to love everybody, but God doesn't have an expectation for white people to examine how they have historically not loved everybody, and then how they perpetuate that non-love in every sphere of this so-called multicultural place? It causes dissonance." —*Black congregant*

Black practicing Christians (33%) feels it is hard to move into a leadership position at a multiracial church. There could be other factors not accounted for here—church size, beliefs about gender roles or organizational structure—that obstruct a path to leadership, whether in multi- or monoracial churches. In looking across all the questions in this series, however, it is clear that some Black Christians face barriers to acceptance or personal growth even when they are in a racially diverse environment.

The data on Black Christians are most stark here; for Asian and Hispanic Christians, experiences of prejudice in a church aren't so related to the congregation's racial or ethnic makeup. This may be because Asian and Hispanic Christians are more likely than Black Christians to attend a language-specific enclave within a multiracial church where they can freely express their cultural identity. But this difference among Black and other non-white groups is also helpful in assessing multiracial churches: If they don't work well for Black individuals, for whom injustices in the U.S. have been deeply felt and particularly injurious, how well do they really work?

Multiracial churches are often previously predominantly white churches that have made an intentional effort to become more diverse. Some of these churches have mostly white leadership (according to attendees of multiracial churches, half have leadership teams that are at least half white. One in four teams is at least 75% white, with 12% being completely white). As a result, the existing norms, traditions, preferences and structures of the church have not significantly changed—except people of color are invited to join. This invitation often comes with an expectation, explicit or implicit, that people of color also *assimilate,* or *fit in* by embracing songs, styles, messages, structures and communities which may be very different from those in their own racial and ethnic culture or previous church tradition.

The expectation that congregants of color assimilate often goes unnoticed by white leaders or attendees because of *white normativity,* or a standard which, explicitly or implicitly, centers white understanding, values and traditions as normal and regards other views as "ethnic," foreign or suspect. For a simple example of this, think about food: In the U.S., people refer to "ethnic food" (Chinese, Thai, Nigerian, etc.) and then just "food." Items that

"It goes back to the idea of assimilation. [The church says], 'We are going to celebrate our ethnic differences, and it is going to be great because we are going to celebrate diversity represented in our campuses, and that will be good enough. We will have one leader of each race and call it done.' It is too shallow; it has the potential to be so much more." —*White congregant*

are accepted as normative remain unlabeled and therefore standard. The same thing can occur within modern worship services—calling out a gospel song or a song performed in Spanish, while leaving contemporary Christian music without designation (see "What Our Worship Preferences Reveal" on page 36 for more).

Our data and focus group interviews affirm the experiences of many people of color who "code switch" to fit in with multiracial faith communities—that is, they feel pressure to dress, speak and otherwise present in a certain way that belies their identity in order to be accepted or taken seriously in a white normative church. Interviewees' accounts show that such compartmentalization of behavior on an ongoing basis can be demoralizing or exhausting for individuals in the racial minority; in trying to fit in this way, they cannot authentically belong.

Furthermore, our focus group participants attest, Christians of color often face barriers to sharing their opinions, whether as a congregant or leader. Even if a multiracial organization brings in leaders of color, these individuals are not usually given real authority or ability to make change. (You can read more about racial dynamics and power-sharing in church leadership on page 111.) White normativity makes it difficult for people of color to feel at home and leads to frustration, discouragement, emotional pain and even spiritual doubt. Those who are unwilling to assimilate are likely to leave or receive signals of unwelcome that cause them to move on.[11] Those who stay help the church achieve a level of statistical diversity, though it may not yet represent true inclusion.

Attitudes About Multi- & Monoracial Worship

The vision of a multiracial church is a compelling one. In addition to scriptural precedents for multiracial worship, modern church leaders see cultivating diversity as an effort to not only bring heaven to earth but also to reflect the world already around them. Strategically (or cynically), diversifying churches may also be seen as a way to combat lower attendance trends in the U.S. Globally, the Church at large is incredibly diverse and decreasingly Western. The Christian population is rapidly growing on every continent, except Europe, North America and Australia, where it is shrinking.[12] Though the U.S. is expected to remain the country with the highest Christian population for some time still, Pew Research Center research shows the shift in the growth of Christianity largely from Europe to the "Global South."

Within the U.S. alone, demographics are evolving. Pastors are taking note that emerging adult generations are more diverse and less religious.[13] Among faith leaders striving to maintain relevance and credibility with increasingly skeptical Millennials and Gen Z, many assume it will be a significant barrier if the nation is multiracial and the Church is not.

Furthermore, multiracial churches are held up as a solution or a sign of hope for how churches can respond to racism or be a part of the healing that is needed. Two-thirds of practicing Christians believe churches, in general, should have a major role in improving race relations in the country. The number-one way they suggest churches should go about doing that? Welcoming people of all races and ethnicities (80%). Overall, and especially among white practicing Christians, those in multiracial churches are more likely to be aware of racial injustice, both past and present, and to feel motivated to address it (see infographic on page 34).

The number-one way practicing Christians suggest churches could improve race relations is by welcoming people of all races and ethnicities.

All said, we can infer that many churches now aspire to be more diverse; the number of multiracial congregations, of *all* faiths, is growing. In 1998, only 6 percent of all places of worship could be described as having at least 20 percent racial or ethnic diversity in their attending membership; as of 2019, just over 20 years later, that proportion had climbed to 16 percent. Within the Christian Church, too, whether Catholic (24%), mainline (11%) or non-mainline (23%), present racial diversity is up from previous decades.[14]

These are perhaps just some of the reasons the vast majority of practicing Christians seems to oppose a monoracial worship environment—specifically, they disagree that "it is helpful to have churches where the races worship separately from one another" (68%).

Through this question alone, we can't know for sure the motivations for the minority who agree it's helpful for different races to worship separately. Some might be malicious—for instance, support of segregation or overt racism.

On the other hand, some in favor of homogeneous worship environments may actually be people of color or supporters of racial

**In Focus:
White Congregants Reexamine Assimilation vs. Accommodation**

"Today, some of us are starting to ask, how do we develop a genuine multiethnic community? ... I would say this is a pivotal year for us, going from assimilation to accommodation."

"I had a realization that somebody summed up for me: 'We don't mind if people of color greet us, entertain us, clean up our trash, but it's something else to say that we're okay with them leading us.'"

"Their way of thinking is going to be different than mine culturally, and I need to respect and value that as opposed to saying, 'Come join the majority culture, and we will make room for you.' This is a huge shift and transformation in my thinking. I would have thought that I was doing the right thing by making shifts and space for letting you be with me, but if the leadership is only white, it's going to stay with that mindset and not change."

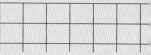

equality who, like some of our focus group participants, feel that monoracial environments serve a unique role in offering support, empowerment and cultural preservation for marginalized communities. As one Black congregant at a Black church shares, "There is freedom in being who I am on a Sunday."

Indeed, we see in the data that Black practicing Christians, followed by Hispanic worshippers, are actually more likely than white practicing Christians to see some value in separate worship. As explored earlier in this chapter, this could be because of the racial prejudice, lack of relational connection and fewer leadership opportunities experienced in multiracial churches. For attendees of color, joining diverse worship environments might mean ceding traditions, influence or preferences.

Despite the positivity around multiracial churches, these data tell us that they are only *part of* a solution when it comes to addressing racism. Not all multiracial churches today promote healthy attitudes about and engagement with issues of race. However, both multi- and monoracial churches, our focus group participants share, can become healthier environments where there

"It is helpful to have churches where the races worship separately from one another"

■ Agree   ⁄⁄⁄ Neutral   ■ Disagree

Practicing Christians
18% 14% 68%

Practicing Christians by race

White
16% 14% 70%

Black
22% 15% 64%

Hispanic
19% 8% 72%

Asian
16% 17% 67%

n=1,364 practicing Christians, July 19–August 5, 2019.

is great spiritual freedom and permission to worship fully and authentically as oneself. Both multi- and monoracial churches have opportunity to grow in justice and unity.

Christians of all stripes have much to learn—and unlearn—when it comes to the topic of race. *Willingness* to learn, the research suggests, is a necessary starting point, as it allows leaders and congregants to overcome ignorance or denial of issues either within their own churches or within the country. Which is why, in the next chapter, we'll go on to assess practicing Christians' awareness of the impact of racism and inequity, in U.S. history and in the present day. ▦

"I was in a men's group with a mix of African American brothers and some white guys, and it was for about a year. ... It was very eye-opening, and I began understanding white privilege and the obstacles that African Americans were up against that I never had to deal with. And relationships began growing from that." ▮

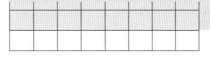

Where Two or More Races Are Gathered

A look at common attitudes and experiences in multiracial and monoracial churches—and how they relate to the churchgoer's own racial identity

When the data point to significant differences in multiracial churches, it is primarily a story that highlights the profound divides between white and Black churchgoers in the U.S. The views and experiences of Hispanic and Asian churchgoers are relatively the same regardless of whether they attend a diverse or homogeneous congregation.

▪ Attendees of multiracial congregations

■ Attendees of monoracial congregations

* statistically significant difference

Views on Racism & Racial Justice

Across multiple questions, white churchgoers in multiracial congregations express greater acknowledgment of racism and motivation to be a part of solutions, compared to their white peers in less diverse churches. Meanwhile, Black churchgoers express the highest concerns about racial justice, no matter where they worship.

"Historically, the United States has been oppressive to minorities"

% agree

48% **38%***	67% **79%**	62% **48%***	38% **38%**
White practicing Christians	**Black** practicing Christians	**Hispanic** practicing Christians	**Asian** practicing Christians

Do you think our country has a race problem?

% "definitely"

45% **34%***	71% **81%**	56% **55%**	36% **39%**
White practicing Christians	**Black** practicing Christians	**Hispanic** practicing Christians	**Asian** practicing Christians

% believe systemic racism is the bigger problem

% believe individual prejudice is the bigger problem

White practicing Christians
31% *
21%
57%
64% *

Black practicing Christians
67%
61%
27%
33%

Hispanic practicing Christians
44%
38%
48%
52%

Asian practicing Christians
35%
25%
54%
53%

Are you motivated to address racial injustice?

% "very motivated" + "motivated"

51% **28%*** 74% **62%** 62% **54%** 40% **17%**

White practicing Christians **Black** practicing Christians **Hispanic** practicing Christians **Asian** practicing Christians

▨ Attendees of multiracial congregations
■ Attendees of monoracial congregations
✱ statistically significant difference

Experiences in Church

White churchgoers report some friction in cross-racial faith communities. Hispanic and Asian churchgoers have consistent experiences in both multiracial and monoracial environments. Black churchgoers, meanwhile, stand out in their reports of barriers in diverse vs. monoracial churches.

% strongly + somewhat agree that they . . .

have experienced racial prejudice | find it difficult to move into leadership positions | find it difficult to build relationships | feel pressure to give up part of their racial / ethnic identity

25%* 9% | 28%* 20% | 25%* 13% | 20%* 6% — **White** practicing Christians

29% 11%* | 33% 16%* | 28% 13%* | 27% 9%* — **Black** practicing Christians

17% 13% | 25% 24% | 26% 20% | 16% 10% — **Hispanic** practicing Christians

16% 11% | 20% 15% | 20% 14% | 10% 5% — **Asian** practicing Christians

n=1,364 practicing Christians, July 19–August 5, 2019.

What Our Worship Preferences Reveal

When talking about cultural differences, preferences pertaining to the style of worship services come up often in interviews and focus groups. The researchers carried that observation into the survey and devised a test to gauge, at a surface level, what a respondent wants in a church leader or in church music. As the survey methodology was conducted online, Barna was able to provide practicing Christian survey takers a variety of stimuli.

Each respondent was presented with a picture of a pastor and a selection of music was played. (Though suggestive, because the pictures are not identical in all ways except race, we must exercise caution in interpreting the findings. Additionally, we did not analyze any images of women as pastors, as views on ordination would likely confound results.) The pairings of pastors and music were random, so that researchers could see a distinct pattern of preferences, as well as the potential trade-offs Christians would be willing or unwilling to make in selecting a church.

Among white practicing Christians, white pastors are preferred, with all music types. White Christians indicate a slight preference for white-led modern worship music (in this case, Hillsong's "Forever"), but are also very likely to consider a church—with a white pastor—that plays gospel music ("I Do Worship" by John P. Kee & The New Life Community Choir) or hymns ("The Old Rugged Cross").

For Black practicing Christians, the gospel song is the favorite, though they are less emphatic about whether they'd prefer a Black (47%) or white (40%) pastor to lead at a church that plays such music.

Bold percentages indicate a group's preferred song pairing only for the pastor pictured. Highlighted percentages indicate a group's preferred song pairing across all pastors. If no percentage is in bold, there was no statistically significant difference.

Songs:

▦ "Forever" by Hillsong
⬤ "I Do Worship" by John P. Kee & The New Life Community Choir
▲ "The Old Rugged Cross"

■ **PREFERENCES** within pastor type
▦ Overall preferences

Pastor	White			Black		
Song type	▦	⬤	▲	▦	⬤	▲
All practicing Christians	**35%**	32%	32%	29%	**32%**	31%
White	**38%**	32%	33%	27%	28%	**30%**
Black	26%	**40%**	32%	39%	**47%**	35%
Hispanic	33%	**36%**	**35%**	33%	**45%**	36%
Asian	**38%**	24%	21%	**29%**	26%	20%

% of practicing Christians who would be "very likely" to attend a church like this. Respondents rated their likelihood to attend for each combination of pastor and music style; they were not forced to pick one.

A similar cultural tradeoff occurs in that Black practicing Christians are equally likely to consider a church that plays Hillsong-style music if the pastor is also Black. In the case of Black practicing Christians, worship preference—for gospel music, specifically—is a more important determinant, over having a pastor who shares their race.

For Hispanic and Asian respondents, it's more difficult to interpret these options through a racial lens, and some styles unique to their traditions or cultures are not represented here. Still, Hispanic practicing Christians tend to choose gospel music, paired with pastors of any race, though they show a preference for a Black pastor. Asian practicing Christians favor modern worship, and preferably with a white pastor.

Following that, they gravitate toward worship under an Asian pastor, with the music of Hillsong or hymns.

There are many intersections in this data; different racial and ethnic groups prioritize leadership identity and music style differently, and this test alone cannot exclusively or exhaustively show which are the strongest predictors in church choice.

This portion of the study, however, paired with insights from qualitative interviews, show a preference for white leadership and worship style in the present-day American Church. For example, the recently conducted Faith Communities Today Study found that 58 percent of megachurches are multiracial. Of these congregations, a shockingly high 94 percent are led by white senior pastors.[15]

Songs:

▦ "Forever" by Hillsong
◍ "I Do Worship" by John P. Kee & The New Life Community Choir
▲ "The Old Rugged Cross"

■ PREFERENCES within pastor type
▦ Overall preferences

Pastor	Hispanic			Asian		
Song type	▦	◍	▲	▦	◍	▲
All practicing Christians	**27%**	26%	25%	25%	24%	25%
White	28%	26%	25%	25%	23%	25%
Black	22%	20%	**28%**	22%	**31%**	22%
Hispanic	23%	**36%**	27%	30%	29%	30%
Asian	**32%**	24%	22%	**33%**	17%	**33%**

n=1,364 practicing Christians, July 19–August 5, 2019.

by David Bailey

CEO AND FOUNDER OF ARRABON

Hospitality, Formation & the 70 Percent Rule

EXPLORING HOW WORSHIP MUSIC SAYS WHO IS WELCOME, SAYS WHO IS A
GUEST AND FORMS A CONGREGATION

I was moderating a panel when I heard my friend Nikki Lerner, a brilliant culture coach, share a thought that remains at the forefront of my mind, particularly each time the topic of hospitality comes up in my presence. Nikki taught me, "Every church has a welcome mat. The question is, does your welcome mat say, 'welcome home' or 'welcome, guest' to people who are different from you?"

Wow! "Welcome home" or "Welcome, guest?"

Any church on mission understands the importance of hospitality, but how many churches think about who they are being hospitable to? There isn't a universal hospitality protocol; what is considered hospitable varies across cultures. So, a church could engage in hospitality in one way that makes one group of people feel like they are at home while making another group of people feel like guests.

Over the last 40 years in church planting movements, one of the key church growth strategies has been what's called the "homogeneous unit principle." This principle upholds the sociological reality that groups tend to gather around shared cultural similarities like education, economics, social, ethnic or racial commonalities. It's easier to grow a church when the "welcome home" mat is set out for people who share a lot of similarities.

At the same time, in the U.S. we hold to the value that every church ought to be self-sustaining. It's worth exploring whether this value is a biblical value or a cultural value. The vast majority of church plants in the last 40 years appears to have operated out of that value, as they have landed in the upper middle class or wealthier zip codes. If you want a self-sustaining church within three years, then it makes sense to plant a church in an upper middle class or higher zip code.

When a church plant is in zip codes with flourishing grade schools and booming shopping centers, the welcome mat is then set out primarily for growing families in the upper middle class. This means the aesthetic, preaching, music and children's ministry are all designed to attract and retain them. Whether consciously or unconsciously, the expression of worship is often decided by the cultural preference of the majority of givers.

Doing church in America is expensive, and, as leaders, it is very easy for us to make fiscal decisions before we make formational decisions. Whether a church is monoracial or multiracial in attendance, those fiscal decisions can consciously or subconsciously cause ministry leaders to make worship decisions based off of the golden rule: "Those that have the gold, make the rules."

"As leaders, it is very easy for us to make fiscal decisions before we make formational decisions."

What if the question around worship shifted to broaden what "welcome home" means? In other words, instead of asking, "What expression of worship will attract our largest giving units?" what if we asked, "How can worship form us to love God and love all of our neighbors?" What if worship formed us to have a diverse perspective of the image of God? What if worship taught us to see and love our neighbor in the way Jesus provocatively taught in the Good Samaritan story? What if worship informed and expanded our hospitality to our neighbor?

A little more than a decade ago, my wife and I became part of a church planting team committed to plant a church that would be diverse racially, ethnically and economically. From the very beginning, we prioritized worship as formation over worship as expression. We didn't discount the importance of the expression of worship. We acknowledged that expressions of worship aren't the same—singing a hymn is not the same as singing a contemporary worship song; singing in one's native tongue isn't the same as singing in a foreign language; singing gospel music isn't the same experience as singing songs from the Taize community. We understood the double truths of who God is and what God requires of us can be expressed in myriad cultural styles. So, we intentionally sought ways to recognize our community's varied expressions of worship.

At some point, we came up with the "70 Percent Rule": if you find yourself comfortable more than 70 percent of the time, something is amiss; your culture is dominating, even in what could be deemed a multicultural church.

Articulating the 70 Percent Rule became a practical way for us to resist forming our community by the gospel of consumer comfort. Some of the most powerful worship we've experienced since occurred when we sang songs of lament written by Urban Doxology during moments of national racial crisis. The 70 Percent Rule has also been good for my own Christian maturity and character. When I struggle to try to connect to God in the midst of my attempts to sing a song in Spanish, I'm reminded of my brother in Christ who came to the U.S. from Mexico at 18 years old and struggled to make a living in a foreign land with a foreign language while I was in college living my best life.

How worship forms us should take priority. Just as singing the words of scripture forms and shapes us, the practice of multicultural expression can form and shape us if we allow it. Both my God-view and my worldview have been shaped by our church endeavoring to set out a welcome mat that says "welcome home" to as many people as possible.

4 Steps to Lead Toward Healthier Multiracial Congregations

Analysis of focus group discussions with members of multiracial churches surfaces a few ways to experience true integration and enhance effectiveness in these faith communities:

1. Acknowledge Differences in Cultures

When churches take a monocultural approach that focuses on one dominant group, attendees in minority groups may see the exclusion of their culture as a rejection of their identities or a signal to assimilate into the majority culture. To prevent this pressure to assimilate, there must be space for each culture represented to be expressed. Cultural differences extend beyond color alone to lived experiences. Education about diversity—in all of its beauty and complexity—can increase empathy, understanding and churchgoers' ability to welcome and love their neighbors. Also helpful for gaining insights to others' cultures is what some call "life on life" groups; they highlight a meaningful difference between actually doing life together (the good and the bad) versus just meeting in the same room.

2. Deal with Race, Not Just Culture

When congregations engage different cultures, perhaps by celebrations of food and music, but leave the power relations of race untouched, they fail to engage in a key area of division. Healthy multiracial churches address systemic inequalities where they exist, acknowledge their effects on the lives of congregants and combat these inequalities within their sphere of influence.

3. Sacrifice Comfort

For a multiracial congregation to resist a culture of assimilation, there comes a time when congregants—specifically those in the racial majority—must become okay with being uncomfortable and embracing reciprocal sacrifice. In welcoming a diverse group of people, a multiracial church should consider whose preferences are permitted to regularly influence the preaching styles and subjects, music selections or service times and lengths. Attendees of healthy multiracial churches speak of the richness of living out inclusion and not just checking the box of statistical diversity.

4. Practice What You Preach

The recommendations above work best when they are intentionally focused on and modeled by leadership. This might include diversifying one's own personal networks and investing time and ministry resources into educational programs that yield common language and priorities around racial justice and create opportunities for quality time with congregants. Pastors in the racial majority may need to prayerfully yield some of their opportunities, responsibilities and preferences in order to submit to or share authority with minority leaders. *See more on page 111, in the section "Who's Got the Mic?"* ∎

2. Then & Now:

Acknowledgment of past and present racial injustice

This report was written during a broad national discussion about racial justice following the killings of George Floyd, Breonna Taylor and other recent instances of police brutality and racist violence. Long-simmering tensions erupted and spurred a series of marches and protests, with participation surpassing the numbers of any movement in U.S. history, including those of the Civil Rights era.[16] The reach and diversity of these demonstrations were unprecedented, but the divides they highlighted are not new.[17]

Our 2019 data, collected months before this surge in discussion of racial justice, show that a majority of the nation's population recognizes a race problem (51% "definitely," 40% "somewhat"). Only 9 percent say this is "not at all" an issue. Practicing Christians, for the most part, agree; nearly half (46%) "definitely" see a race problem in the country, with another two in five (43%) saying this is "somewhat" the case and just one in 10 rejecting this idea (11% "not at all"). Certainty of racism's impact increases among those who aren't religious, however; three in five of those who identify as having no faith (60%) "definitely" affirm it's a problem.

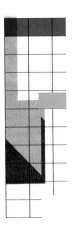

There are further differences by racial group among practicing Christians that start to provide context around disparities, including those in multiracial churches. Only two in five white practicing Christians (38%) believe the U.S. "definitely" has a race problem. This percentage more than doubles, however, among Black practicing Christians (78%). Their Hispanic peers follow close behind, with over half (56%) noting a problem. By comparison, Asian practicing Christians are less confident (38% "definitely," 51% "somewhat") there is a problem, though white Christians are the most likely racial category to say, "not at all" (13%).

Do you think our country has a race problem?

U.S adults by faith segment

■ Definitely   ■ Somewhat   ■ Not at all

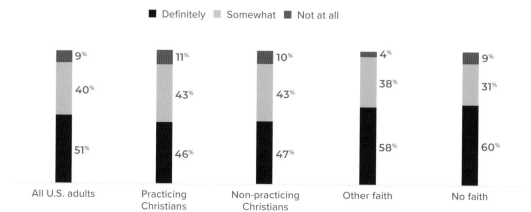

n=1,525 U.S. adults, July 19–August 5, 2019.
n=1,364 practicing Christians, July 19–August 5, 2019.

Practicing Christians by race

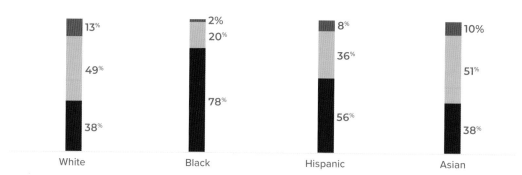

n=1,364 practicing Christians, July 19–August 5, 2019.

Barna had the opportunity to revisit this question in a summer 2020 survey—and found that these divides had only deepened in the midst of the nationwide outcry against racial injustice. There is actually a significant increase in the percentage of practicing Christians who say race is "not at all" a problem in the U.S., to 19 percent, led by white Christians. In other words, many Christians took steps backward or became more resistant to calls for racial justice after the summer of 2020. (The 2020 study does not have a large enough sample of practicing Christians to compare across all racial categories, as we do in this report. For comparisons by race among all self-identified Christians, refer to Barna's *Race Today* study.)

It's concerning that white Christians' acknowledgment of the burdens borne by other racial groups is remarkably low—and remained so even as protests, advocacy and awareness initiatives intensified.

These conflicting responses emphasize why diversity alone is not enough: It's important to understand different racial groups' perspectives, rather than looking only at the average, in which white perspectives dominate. Further, it's concerning that white Christians' acknowledgment of the burdens borne by other racial groups is remarkably low—and remained so even as protests, advocacy and awareness initiatives intensified.

That concern deepens when we consider data show a majority of all Christians, of all races, believes the Church should play a major role in addressing race relations. If white Christians are so much less likely to acknowledge such issues presently exist, it follows that they are unlikely to assume an organizational role in addressing it.

Awareness of Present-Day Discrimination & Inequity

Black, Hispanic and Asian Americans in this study attest to the experience of navigating biased systems and laws, and public statistics and reports enumerate the economic and legal inequality facing people of color in the U.S. (see page 55). But white adults, and white Christians in particular, aren't convinced this is so; some tend to emphasize their own personal hardships instead. They may be unaware of disadvantages for people of color—or they may be minimizing them. They may be overly optimistic about existing inequities—or, consciously or unconsciously, denying them.

As we will go on to explore in the following chapter, their views on racial justice and equality are primarily formed by an individualized, rather than systemic or structural, perspective. This perspective may produce the inability to see inequality even in light of evidence.[18]

White Perceptions of How People of Color Are Treated in the U.S.

In general, in our country these days, would you say that ....

■ White practicing Christians
■ Other white U.S. adults

	In hiring, pay and promotions	When applying for a loan or mortgage	By the courts and justice systems
Black people are treated less fairly than white people	39% / 49%	33% / 43%	49% / 59%
White people are treated less fairly than Black people	14% / 12%	7% / 9%	7% / 7%
Both are treated equally	47% / 39%	60% / 49%	44% / 34%
Hispanic people are treated less fairly than white people	20% / 22%	14% / 19%	17% / 19%
White people are treated less fairly than Hispanic people	9% / 9%	9% / 7%	7% / 7%
Both are treated equally	71% / 68%	77% / 73%	76% / 74%
Asian / Asian American people are treated less fairly than white people	45% / 53%	38% / 48%	42% / 51%
White people are treated less fairly than Asian / Asian American people	12% / 11%	9% / 9%	8% / 8%
Both are treated equally	43% / 36%	52% / 43%	50% / 41%

n=720 U.S. white practicing Christians, 831 all other U.S. white adults, July 19–August 5, 2019.

Let's get specific. A series of questions in the survey explore perceptions of manifestations of inequity or discrimination in jobs, housing or in the legal and justice system. In each of these areas, respondents compare the treatment of racial minorities to that of white Americans. At this point in the report, we'll focus on those perceptions among white Americans themselves, as they most starkly demonstrate contrasting views in the U.S. and the Church. However, it is worth noting that Black adults are most likely to affirm inequities in each of these areas (usually around eight in 10 say they have it worse than white people), followed by Hispanic adults (about two-thirds point to hardships). Most Asian Americans say they are treated about equally in the housing or legal system, but when it comes to jobs, about half say they are at a disadvantage. As previously pointed out, there is ample secondary evidence supporting these observations of inequities. *See the data tables in the Appendix for more on how people of color view the treatment of various racial groups.*

When white respondents do acknowledge racial discrimination in these systems, they believe Black and Hispanic adults are more likely than Asians to be victims of discrimination. They see Black adults especially receiving worse treatment in the courts and justice system. Similar percentages of all white adults say Black and Hispanic people do not receive fair treatment when it comes to seeking jobs, pay and promotions or in applying for a loan or mortgage. In all of these areas, a consistent majority feels there is no real difference between how Asian adults and white adults are treated.

There is a direct correlation between white American Christian identity and rejection of the reality of past racial oppression.

Christian identity, however, proves to be a significant factor in white views of discrimination. In every scenario presented—professional, economic, legal—white practicing Christians are more likely than all other white adults to say individuals of color are treated similarly to white people. Given popular discussion and documentation of racial injustices within the courts and justice system, especially in regard to how Black men are treated, it is noteworthy that Christians' perceptions are so inaccurate—especially when the majority of all other white U.S. adults (59% vs. 49% white practicing Christians) sees this as a clear example of racial disparity in America.

Some white practicing Christians also perpetuate a narrative of "reverse racism," or the perceived unfair treatment of white adults, specifically in the context of jobs and pay. Though this is a marginal view, it is backed in focus group answers, in which a number of white practicing Christians, men in particular, assert their own financial struggles, stress how hard they have worked and express some concern about Black Americans getting preferential treatment in jobs and college admissions. Their discussion of this perceived financial threat was emotional, sometimes visceral.

Some corners of the Church are more willing to acknowledge inherent racial inequities. We know from more than a decade of research that younger generations have a bent toward social justice, and indeed, practicing Christian Gen Z and Millennials are often significantly more likely than older age groups to say that racial minorities are treated less fairly than white people.

It is generally accepted that younger generations are more attuned to and more motivated to work toward racial justice. Regression analysis, however, reveals that, while age is a predictive factor of acknowledging discrimination, it is not significantly correlated with identifying what discriminatory systems look like, such as recorded racial disparities in hiring and criminal justice. Other research affirms that young white people, though aware of and angered by racism, do not seem to notice specific markers of their own advantages or the disadvantages of people of color.[19]

Gen Z and Millennials may feel their general acknowledgment of racial inequity is the "right" answer, but they still require education on what it looks like in practice. In other words, Christians cannot passively hope that racial injustice will be slowly eliminated and unity will be achieved by younger generations gaining in maturity and influence.

Looking Back: Awareness of Historic Oppression

Clearly, there is a divide in recognition of *present* problems. To what degree are Americans aware of *past* mistreatment of different racial groups?

In this study, half of U.S. adults (50%), including practicing Christians (48%), agree to some extent that the nation has, historically, been oppressive to minorities. Yet, by faith segment, practicing Christians are less likely to agree *strongly* with this statement (20%), and more than one-quarter of practicing Christians (27%) disagrees. Those of other faiths generally acknowledge (35% somewhat agree) a history of racial mistreatment, while the plurality of those of

continued on page 53

Raymond Chang

PRESIDENT AND CO-FOUNDER OF
ASIAN AMERICAN CHRISTIAN COLLABORATIVE

Racial Justice in Asian American Experience

The first Asians to place their feet on North American soil were recorded to have done so in the late 1500s. The first Asians to establish a settlement ("Manila men") did so on the outskirts of New Orleans by 1763. They were sailors from the Philippines. However, it wasn't until the 1800s when Asian immigration really began to increase in more significant ways. Sadly, it only took a few decades for white nativist hostility to intensify, which would lead the U.S. government to take steps to exclude Asians from immigration, naturalization and full citizenship. Starting with the Chinese Exclusion Act of 1882, race-based immigration policies were established for nearly 80 years, preventing Asians from entering into the U.S. It wasn't until 1965, the same year the Voting Rights Act was passed to prohibit racial discrimination in voting, that naturalization laws were changed. From experiencing life as "coolies" (laborers) to discrimination, harassment and racism (including the Chinese massacre of 1871, the largest mass lynching to take place in the U.S.), Asian Americans have endured a lot of pain.

In some ways, the racism we have experienced overlaps with the Black and Brown experience in America. In other ways, specific manifestations of racism against Asian Americans differ significantly. Nonetheless, any serious study of history will reveal that the racism Black, Brown, First Nation and Asian Americans have faced and currently face is similarly rooted in white supremacy. White supremacy is also ultimately responsible for cultivating longstanding inter-minority tensions and conflicts between our communities—including between Black and Asian Americans.

Inter-Minority Tensions

All this is to say, Asian Americans have our own disconcerting history when it comes to racism and racialization. Asians were first brought to the United States as replacement labor for African slaves. I'd like to say this has made Black and Asian Americans

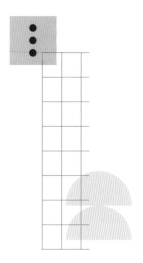

natural allies in pursuit of societal justice, but instead, it has often led to inter-minority tensions due to a lack of understanding around the ways race functions and how white supremacy operates. This confusion has led many to falsely believe that the tensions developed out of our own isolated issues, not the result of the larger racial framework of white supremacy that has pitted Asians and Black Americans against each other.

A common narrative one might hear from Asian Americans, especially those from older generations, is that they've experienced pain at the hands of African Americans. Asian Americans bought into the "American dream" (which followed the mythical promises of riches of "gold mountain" that lured many Chinese laborers to the U.S.). Throughout history, but especially after the 1965 Immigration Act, as Asians arrived in the U.S., they quickly realized that they weren't welcome in white neighborhoods and business districts. So, many went where there was more openness to opportunity and started businesses in largely under-resourced Black and Brown neighborhoods, which contributed to the riots and boycotts of the early 1990s in Los Angeles and New York. Many Asian business owners lost their livelihoods, causing a painful touchpoint in our histories. Language and cultural barriers led to a lot of misunderstandings and, to a degree, hindered the cultivation of cross-racial community building. But, more significantly, a white supremacist framework dominated the racial understandings that community members had of one another.

Asians bought into the idea that if they kept their heads down, worked hard, got a good education and didn't complain or draw attention to themselves, they would be able to carve out a comfortable living for themselves and their children. In part, this is how the "model minority" myth was born. Asians believed the false notion that if they came to the United States, they could plant their feet and flourish. What they didn't realize is that they entered into a context where generations of systemic racial injustice left African American communities severely under-resourced. Additionally, the racist stereotypes developed by a white supremacist racial logic preceded both of the communities in their interactions. In order to keep Asians down and out, they were portrayed as outside invaders who were "filthy," "dirty" and "yellow peril." These were the messages many had heard about Asians, which often fueled negative interactions.

However, in a white supremacist framework where white is "good" and Black is "bad," there is no space for others—which is why racism against Asians and Latinos and Native Americans often flies under the radar.

Stories of hurt come from Black community members as well. Oftentimes, Asians came into their neighborhoods to open up a nail salon, a liquor store or a bodega, but didn't reinvest in and become part of the community. Many African Americans believed Asians were siphoning money out of their community and spending it in another, brewing animosity and prejudice. Though there is some truth to this narrative, what it fails to capture is how often Asian businesses barely survived, relying on the free or cheap labor of their family members (including their children) to get by, meaning that there was little money available to reinvest into any community. When Asian American business did "succeed," it often came at great emotional, mental, physical and relational (familial) cost.

"In a racial framework where white is on top and everyone is beneath, non-white communities are led to believe they are in competition with one another to the detriment of inter-minority solidarity and unity."

Sadly, some of the most pervasive narratives don't tell the many stories of cooperation and genuine friendship or efforts to provide scholarships and summer camps (often led by churches and community members seeking to heal the racial divides that whiteness created). Rarely do you hear the stories of how Korean American merchants sponsored sports teams and held picnics to reach out to local communities. Even rarer in the public eye are the stories of decades-long friendships that have endured through all the racial tensions because members from both communities committed to deep and enduring friendships with one another.

What's difficult is that in a racial framework where white is on top and everyone is beneath, non-white communities are led to believe they are in competition with one another to the detriment of inter-minority solidarity and unity. The false promises of an honorary white status often lead us to believe that we should pursue whiteness (or whatever is closest to whiteness) instead of seeking to uplift each other's causes. The pursuit of racial dominance through the promotion and preservation of white normativity is not consistent with Christian values and a Christian ethic where we are called to seek the interest of others and to care for those that Jesus would have cared for—especially the marginalized and the oppressed.

Just the Beginning

I serve as president of the Asian American Christian Collaborative, where we're trying to change this dynamic and bring about healing. In the summer of 2020, we hosted an Asian American–led Christian march for Black lives through Chicago, a city that's been segregated by ethnicity as a matter of government policy from very early on in its history. Up to 2,000 people (mostly Asian American) representing

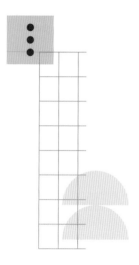

over 100 churches started in Chinatown and marched from a historic Chinese church (Chinese Christian Union Church) to a historic African American Church (Progressive Baptist Church), praying that God's Spirit would break strongholds of racism, prejudice and injustice in the city, the nation and the world. As we journeyed through the physical city, we also took a spiritual journey of lament, grief, confession and repentance, ending in prayerful commitment to a Christ-centered unity and pursuit of justice.

It was a beautiful, powerful experience—but it was just a beginning.

When you look across the country at various movements, conferences and conversations related to racial justice and reconciliation, it's almost always a Black-and-white dialogue. If there are Latino- or Asian- or Native Americans, they tend to be on the periphery. Our organization and others like us want to complicate and complexify the conversation because, only by acknowledging the complexity of racism in America can we take meaningful steps toward untangling its powerful web. We want to educate and empower Asian Christians to stand in solidarity with our Black and Brown sisters and brothers, and invite Black, Latino, Native and white Christians to stand in solidarity with Asian American believers. No Christian, no matter his or her ethnicity, should be comfortable hearing the president of the United States call COVID-19 the "Chinese virus" or "kung flu" when we have a long history of anti-Asian hate grounded in notions of Asians being "yellow peril."

Anti-Asian racism is real and rising. A few months ago, during the pandemic lockdown, I was sitting on my front porch. A white driver rolled down his window and screamed, calling me a "yellow piece of [expletive]." All he knew about me was that I had "Asian" features. All I could think was, "Now that guy knows where I live. Will he come back later? Is my wife safe here?" All I could think about was how all throughout history, Asians were seen as a virus invading, infesting and sickening America. And now here we were again. Over the course of the pandemic, we have seen our youth and elderly shoved, spit on, slashed and stabbed.

As fellow citizens in God's Kingdom, we belong to a multiethnic, multicultural, multilingual family bound together by his Spirit. That beloved community (as Dr. King called it) must be our first allegiance. There were many costs associated with leaving the familiar ancestral lands of Korea, even after the country was ravaged by war, and I am grateful for my parents' many sacrifices. But I am especially grateful that in everything I do, I am encouraged by them to pursue the Kingdom of God above all else. I am encouraged that, even through their many sacrifices, they know that followers of Jesus must always turn to the margins, to the corners of society where people are ignored or left behind. ▦

Adapted from an interview with Chad Brennan. Used by permission.

continued from page 48

no faith (33% strongly agree, 26% somewhat agree) is emphatic that this oppression has existed.

On the whole, there is a direct correlation between white American Christian identity and denial of the reality of past racial oppression. When pairing race and faith, we see that Black practicing Christians are insistent—more so even than other Black respondents—that the U.S. has perpetrated racial oppression (44% strongly agree). Hispanic and Asian practicing Christians trend toward the center of the spectrum of agreement. Meanwhile, only one in seven white practicing Christians (14%) strongly agrees the U.S. has a track record of being oppressive to minorities. Together, with those who somewhat agree (28%), less than half support this reading of history. Notably, one in three white practicing Christians either strongly (19%) or somewhat disagrees (14%) there has historically been oppression of minorities, a much higher percentage than other groups.

Overall, these data represent an unwillingness on the part of some groups to admit basic realities of the country's history. According to a 2019 study by faculty members at Yale University's School of Management, Department of Psychology and Institute for Social and Policy Studies, this is a common phenomenon in which groups who have benefited from the historic oppression of other groups are conditioned to focus on the positives rather than negatives,

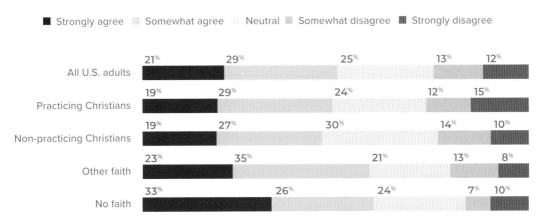

"Historically, the U.S. has been oppressive to minorities"

U.S. adults by faith segment

■ Strongly agree ▨ Somewhat agree ▨ Neutral ▨ Somewhat disagree ■ Strongly disagree

	Strongly agree	Somewhat agree	Neutral	Somewhat disagree	Strongly disagree
All U.S. adults	21%	29%	25%	13%	12%
Practicing Christians	19%	29%	24%	12%	15%
Non-practicing Christians	19%	27%	30%	14%	10%
Other faith	23%	35%	21%	13%	8%
No faith	33%	26%	24%	7%	10%

n=1,525 U.S. adults, July 19–August 5, 2019.
n=1,364 practicing Christians, July 19–August 5, 2019.

diminishing the perceived impact of injustices: "We have a strong and persistent belief that our national disgrace of racial oppression has been overcome, albeit through struggle, and that racial equality has largely been achieved. ... Most Americans hold an unyielding belief in a specific, optimistic narrative regarding racial progress that is robust to counterexamples: that society has come a very long way already and is moving rapidly, perhaps naturally toward full racial equality."[20]

Many religious leaders in the space of racial justice—including individuals and experts interviewed for this project—propose it will be nearly impossible for the Church to play a role in racial justice if there is little recognition of past racial injustice.

There has been some movement in this area: In the summer 2020 survey, Barna re-asked this question of whether the U.S. has, historically, oppressed minorities. This time, we saw a boost in practicing Christians' willingness to strongly agree—from 19 percent in the 2019 survey that informs this study, to 32 percent in the summer of 2020. This year-over-year trend occurred among white Christians as well, who joined their peers of other races in becoming significantly more likely to agree and significantly less likely to disagree that minorities have faced oppression.

"Historically, the U.S. has been oppressive to minorities"

Practicing Christians by race

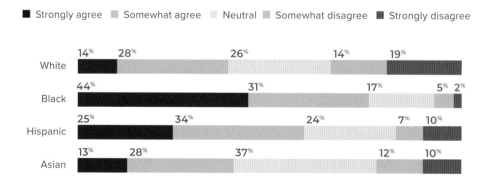

n=1,364 practicing Christians, July 19–August 5, 2019.

The Facts of Inequity

A wealth of public research and records reveal that discrimination and disadvantage exist on more than just a personal level and are complex, widespread and deep-seated. Recently, for example, the U.S. has witnessed this in the disproportionate impact of COVID-19 in non-white populations, likely due to other socioeconomic factors such as access to health care and increased occupational exposure. For instance, Black adults make up 13 percent of the U.S. population, but 23 percent of all COVID deaths.[21]

INCOME[22]

- The typical white family has eight times the wealth of the typical Black family and five times the wealth of the typical Hispanic family.
- White families have the highest level of median wealth: $188,200. Black families' median wealth is $24,100. Hispanic families' median wealth is $36,100.
- Nearly 30 percent of white families report having received an inheritance or gift, compared to about 10 percent of Black families and 7 percent of Hispanic families.
- Even when they both have a bachelor's degree, a white man still makes, on average, $7 more an hour than a Black man.
- Despite graduating from college at higher rates, Asian Americans are less likely than white Americans to be promoted or hired to senior-level roles.

EDUCATION[23]

- Nearly one-third of Hispanic adults (31%) never completed high school. Only one in four Black adults (26%) has a bachelor's degree or higher, compared to 40 percent of white adults and 58 percent of Asians.
- Socioeconomic status (specifically, the intersection of education, income and wealth) is one of the largest predictors of educational success—meaning, those born wealthy perform better in school and those born into poverty perform worse. As Black and Hispanic individuals are disproportionally likely to live in poverty, there is a cyclical educational inequity.
- On average, by the fourth grade, white children outscore Black and Hispanic children by 32 and 27 points (respectively).
- Children eligible for free lunch—more likely to be people of color—score 28 points lower on reading and 24 points lower on math, on average, than those not eligible for free lunch.
- Black male children are three times more likely to receive out-of-school suspension than white male children.

HOUSING[24]

- At the time of the housing market crash in 2008, 68 percent of adults owned their home. This included 75 percent of white adults and 47 percent of Black adults. White adults have regained most of what they lost since then, while Black adults are actually in a worse position.
- In 2019, two-thirds of Americans (65%) owned their home. Seven out of 10 white adults (73%) owned their house, compared to only 42 percent of Black adults and 48 percent of Hispanic adults. Black Americans are the least likely race group to own their home.
- In 2019, approximately 9.4 million Americans were living in public housing. Of them, two in three (66%) were part of an ethnic minority and 44 percent were Black.
- Of adults renting their home, 58 percent are Black. This number has risen about 7 percentage points since 2014.

INCARCERATION[25]

- Even though white Americans make up 4.5 times more of the U.S. population, Black Americans make up a higher proportion of the prison population. Of all prisoners, 33 percent are Black (vs. 30% white and 23% Hispanic).
- The U.S. makes up 5 percent of the world's population, but 25 percent of the world's prison population. A white male has a one in 17 chance of being incarcerated, while a Black male has a one in three chance.
- As of 2016, one in nine inmates was serving a life sentence, one-third of whom had no chance at parole. Half of this population segment was Black.
- The odds of receiving a plea offer that includes jail time are almost 70 points greater for Black adults compared to white adults. ▮

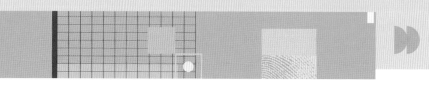

Dominique DuBois Gilliard

DIRECTOR OF RACIAL RIGHTEOUSNESS &
RECONCILIATION FOR THE EVANGELICAL COVENANT
CHURCH; AUTHOR OF *RETHINKING INCARCERATION*

Practicing Remembrance & Proximity

If Christians take seriously Jesus' words recorded in Matthew 25, we follow him and get close to people suffering the pain of injustice and systemic sin. The more intentional we are about drawing close to people in pain—from sickness, hunger, incarceration—the deeper our understanding of the gospel's call on our lives. What does it actually look like to practice communing with the least of these as Jesus commands us to do?

The first practice is to *remember*. In the Old Testament, God commands his people nearly 100 times to remember. Remembrance is the linchpin for Israel's faithfulness—and forgetting always sets them on the road to unfaithfulness. So long as they make a practice of remembering that God liberated them from slavery, they don't enact enslavement on others. But when they forget …

I believe the Church must practice remembrance, just as Israel was commanded to do. Like Israel, we too easily forget who we are and *whose* we are, making us prone to create systems and structures that marginalize some and privilege others. But remembering, regularly and corporately, is a spiritual practice that grounds us in reality and compels us to confession and repentance. It re-roots us in our identity as people who are called to walk the narrow way and live into our citizenship that is not of this world.

Practically speaking, churches can engage in a regular practice of remembrance. Four, six, 12 times a year—whatever rhythm is sustainable—gather to remember events and times when the Church, confronted with injustice, has been silent, complicit or culpable. For example, FDR signed Executive Order 9066 on February 19, 1942, which authorized internment camps for Japanese immigrants and citizens. For the most part, the Church did not speak out against it; in many cases, we supported that unjust policy. June 17 is the anniversary of the Mother Emanuel shooting, in which nine worshippers were murdered by a

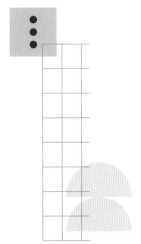

white supremacist. How has the Church been complicit in tolerating or even inflaming a racist, anti-Christ ideology? On May 4, 1493, Pope Alexander VI issued a papal bull authorizing what's come to be known as the "doctrine of discovery," charging Christians to take possession of all lands inhabited by non-Christians. How are we grappling with and making amends for the violence and genocide at the heart of that legacy?

Practicing remembrance together gives the Church an opportunity to say, "These are the ways we have missed the mark. We recognize that we are continually tempted, and confess that we are sometimes seduced, to conform to the patterns and logic of this world. This act of remembrance keeps us mindful of how we fall short and of our commitment to faithfully follow Jesus against the world's coercion. We will discern what is right and true and good through the power of the Holy Spirit."

The second practice is to *draw close* to those who are suffering injustice. Where are the suffering people in my context? How can I draw close to them? How do I grow relationships with people impacted by injustices that often are reduced to political issues? When we begin cultivating relationships, we see that these are not only political challenges. There's good theology at stake, as well.

A lot of my work revolves around the criminal justice system. According to Jesus' command in Matthew 25, that's where Christians are supposed to be. He doesn't qualify it; he doesn't say, "If you're a liberal, be present with the prisoner." He says the sheep who follow him visit those who are incarcerated. Hebrews tells us to "remember those in prison, as if you were there yourself" (13:3). In a nation with more people incarcerated than any other country in the history of the world, what would it look like if the Church actually did this?

"These are not only political challenges. There's good theology at stake, as well."

When people wonder how to get started, I tell them to call up the closest carceral facility—jail, prison, detention center—and ask to speak to the chaplain: "How can we support you? We are commissioned by Christ to actively engage people in our criminal justice system, and we want to obey him. We want to promote and participate in prisoners' opportunities for transformation, lasting rehabilitation and healthy reintegration into community. How can we help?" That is enacting good theology.

For many Christians, Black Lives Matter is a charged or even offensive movement. But at the heart, "Black lives matter" is prophetic proclamation, a theological statement, and I challenge Christians to hear it that way. Black lives matter says aloud that our world is not as it should be, not as God intended, and connecting with the anguish of those who lament is a theological act. Philippians 2 tells us to agree wholeheartedly with each other, to love one another and to work together with one mind and purpose: What would be our response to BLM if we took a Philippians 2 posture? Ephesians 6 reminds us that our enemies are not flesh and blood but rather we wrestle against powers, principalities and spiritual wickedness in high places: What would be our response to BLM if we took Ephesians seriously?

When it comes to evangelism, to proclaiming Jesus is Lord and his Kingdom is coming, those who are most in need of good news are people in pain, people in despair. Drawing close in solidarity is how we bear witness to the coming Kingdom. ▦

Adapted from an interview with Chad Brennan. Used by permission.

3. "We" & "Me:"

Perspectives regarding systemic racism and individual prejudice

Thus far in this report, we've been circling two understandings of racism—individual and systemic. Tackling these complex terms is necessary in order to move beyond symbolic diversity toward holistic racial justice, as they are wrapped up in how Christians see themselves, their fellow worshippers, their communities and the country.

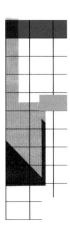

Where individual prejudice involves a person's biased opinions, systemic racism involves how organizations, laws and institutions discriminate against people of color. These forces of injustice are not mutually exclusive, though, as you'll see, there is disagreement about which poses a greater threat. Accordingly, there are very different solutions proposed to end these different forms of inequity.

Addressing individual prejudice might mean focusing on a message of unity and inclusion, building personal relationships across races, confronting prejudicial behaviors or examining unconscious bias. Addressing systemic racism might mean grappling with broader national histories and structures, such as the fallout of redlining, gerrymandering, voter-ID laws, education systems built on property taxes and other institutions and policies that, intentionally or not, benefit white people and leave people of color at a disadvantage. In a church context, addressing individual prejudice might mean cultivating healthy diversity, breaking bread together, engaging in personal repentance and emphasizing oneness in Christ. Addressing systemic racism might mean correcting harmful theologies, changing funding models or denominational policies that (implicitly or explicitly) reinforce white normativity and resourcing churches and institutions that offer acceptance, opportunity and influence for worshippers and leaders of color.

In diverse community, the same word can have many connotations. "Systemic racism and individual prejudice" are technical, charged and politicized terms that may require explanation for some Christians and prompt great debate for most; we see this both in the research and in present public discourse. The survey does not use these terms explicitly—however, respondents were asked more plainly: *Which is the bigger problem in the U.S. today: individuals' own beliefs and prejudices that cause them to treat people of other races poorly, or racial discrimination that is historically built into our society and institutions?*

As noted in the previous chapter, over the course of one year, there were notable shifts in ideas about whether the U.S. has a race problem or has historically oppressed minorities. On this question, however, perceptions held steady between 2019 and 2020 and saw no statistically significant changes: About one-third of U.S. adults (34%, including 33% of practicing Christians) believes the locus of our race problems is systemic, a product of historical and institutional discrimination.

The more common belief, however, is that racial tensions are principally driven by individual beliefs and prejudices. Just over half (52% of the general population, 55% of practicing Christians) say individual prejudice is the

Which of the following do you think is the bigger problem in the United States today?

■ Individuals' own beliefs and prejudices that cause them to treat people of other races poorly
▨ Racial discrimination that is historically built into our society and institutions
▨ Don't know

All U.S. adults: 52% | 34% | 14%
Practicing Christians: 55% | 33% | 12%

n=1,525 U.S. adults, July 19–August 5, 2019.
n=1,364 practicing Christians, July 19–August 5, 2019.

We & Me 63

bigger problem today. About one-eighth doesn't know which form of discrimination is more severe (14% of the general population, 12% of practicing Christians).

The more common belief is that racial tensions are principally driven by the prejudices of individuals who treat people of other races poorly.

There are many reasons individual prejudice is the go-to narrative. One factor may simply be that it is, well, simpler. If enactment of prejudice on a personal level is seen as the driving force behind racism, there is a tendency to dismiss, dissociate from or delegate problems outside of one's periphery and to focus instead on situations and solutions in one's control, relationships and context. This dissociation, however, allows systemic issues to fester.

Systemic racial injustice requires more complex solutions because it highlights the racism built into the foundations of structures, some long-established, and examines one's involvement or complicity within them. For example, undoing residential segregation would require addressing discrimination in banking, real estate, education, the economy and other social institutions, not just addressing interpersonal prejudice among residents and neighbors. Such a systemic response might entail pushing for or hoping in government intervention or legislation, which might not come naturally to most practicing Christians—who, we know from the data, lean politically conservative and tend to look to individuals (84%) or churches (64%) to address race relations before they look to the government to do so (55%).

Importantly, we must consider the dramatic disconnect between different racial groups on the more significant cause of racism in the U.S. Three in five white practicing Christians (61%) take an individualized approach to matters of race, saying these issues largely stem from one's own beliefs and prejudices causing them to treat people of other races poorly. Meanwhile, two-thirds of Black practicing Christians (67%) agree that the greater danger is racial discrimination that is historically built into our society and institutions. Hispanics are fairly split (49% individual, 44% systemic), and Asian practicing Christians are more likely to believe individual prejudice is the greater problem (59%). It is no wonder, then, that churches striving

Which of the following do you think is the bigger problem in the United States today?

Practicing Christians by race

▓ Racial discrimination that is historically built into our society and institutions
■ Individuals' own beliefs and prejudices that cause them to treat people of other races poorly
▒ Don't know

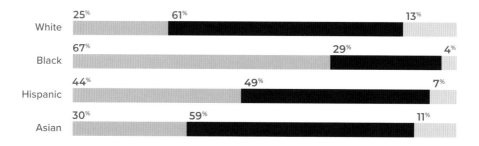

White   25%   61%   13%
Black   67%   29%   4%
Hispanic   44%   49%   7%
Asian   30%   59%   11%

n=1,364 practicing Christians, July 19–August 5, 2019.

Practicing Christians by generation

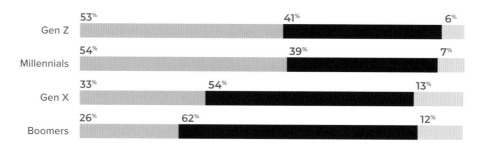

Gen Z   53%   41%   6%
Millennials   54%   39%   7%
Gen X   33%   54%   13%
Boomers   26%   62%   12%

n=1,364 practicing Christians, July 19–August 5, 2019.

for diversity and unity across races still struggle to succeed in reconciling; even in coming together, the measure of the problems and how to achieve progress are not the same.

Across practicing Christian generations, we see a chasm on this question—with Gen Z and Millennials on one side, and Gen X and Boomers on the other. The former are more concerned about institutional discrimination, and the latter are more concerned about individual prejudice. It's possible some of those in the Boomer generation feel they have already witnessed progress in addressing systemic injustice over the years, through initiatives likes the Civil Rights Act, school desegregation and affirmative action. Younger adults, however, see more, and sweeping, work to be done. Even those with differing opinions on these matters must conclude that the major generational gap between younger and older practicing Christians will require clear and cogent Christian leadership.

Even in coming together, the measure of the problems and how to achieve progress are not the same.

Interestingly, having a small percentage of leaders of color at a church does not mean congregants are more likely to feel the weight of current or historical racism. An example: Barna looked at the opinions of practicing Christians in churches (multiracial and otherwise) where leadership teams are said to be completely white (100%), compared to teams said to have predominantly but not completely white staffs (80%–99%). Churchgoers in both of these types of congregations have largely the same views as one another when it comes to race: They're unlikely to see a problem, and if they do, they typically regard it as personal. In other words, even when one or a few leaders of color are on staff, that slight diversity in leadership isn't a guarantee of diverse views in the pews.

To be clear, we can't examine the reported composition of church leadership as the *cause* of popular perspectives of congregations—but these correlations point to contexts where leaders of color are likely to be tokenized or working in an environment of white normativity. (In chapter 6, we'll look more at how the racial identity of church leaders correlates with the experiences of congregants.)

Views on Race in Churches with Completely or Mostly White Leadership	100% white staff	80% white staff
Historically, the United States has been oppressive to minorities (% strongly agree)	13%	13%
Our country "definitely" has a race problem	39%	40%
The bigger problem is racial discrimination that is historically built into our society and institutions	27%	21%
The bigger problem is individuals' own beliefs and prejudices that cause them to treat people of other races poorly	56%	68%

n=588 practicing Christians attending a church with at least 80% white leadership, July 19–August 5, 2019.

Stereotypes Surrounding Inequity

Digging deeper, survey respondents were asked to identify and rank reasons that Black, Hispanic or Asian Americans, statistically, experience different treatment than white Americans. The goal here was to see not just whether people perceive these gaps—as we first explored in chapter two—but also *why* they think these gaps exist.

Some of the responses provided dismiss a systemic dimension to racial disparity, lean on negative stereotypes or claim racial inequity does not exist. Such views are selected most among white practicing Christians, when compared with members of the racial groups referenced in the questions. Those who might witness or personally experience these inequities are more inclined to mention their institutional roots, while white Christians are more inclined to fault individual failures.

This pattern surfaces most clearly and troublingly when we look at how Black and white Christians rank the obstacles facing Black people. (More responses among all racial groups can be found in the Appendix, on page 132.) First of all, one-fifth of white practicing Christians does not believe Black people experience disadvantages in regard to jobs, housing and income. Among those who do accept this fact, they see the top drivers of

continued on page 72

Dorena Williamson

AUTHOR OF *COLORFULL*, *THOUGHTFULL*
AND *GRACEFULL*; CO-PLANTER OF
STRONG TOWER BIBLE CHURCH

Q&A

Educating the Next Generation About Race

Q. **There is a lot of talk right now about raising kids to be aware of and resistant to racism. What role, if any, do you think churches should or could play?**

A. Churches can be a powerful training partner for helping families raise antiracist kids. While race as a human construct is a few hundred years old, we see structural inequity between people groups all through the Bible. Egyptian taskmasters were cruel and intimidating toward their Hebrew slaves in the book of Exodus. Widowed Ruth and Naomi socially benefitted from gleaning, established as a system of care for the marginalized in the Israel community. Members of the early church sold possessions and gave so there was no lack in the community of believers. Ethnic leaders were appointed to address the disparity among Greek-speaking Jewish widows who were being overlooked in Acts. These biblical themes of justice, oppression and equity are all connected to the active work of antiracism. Church leaders can highlight these biblical stories with modern-day parallels to ongoing race-based injustice.

Churches are also the perfect place to teach a bigger picture of God's diverse Kingdom. As a haven of education and empowerment for enslaved Africans who were excluded from houses of worship, the formation of the Black Church in America is a model of antiracism. Children should learn about this history, as well as the stories of ethnically diverse believers undergoing oppression around the world today.

Ecclesiastes 5:8 is a great template for training antiracist youth. Teach by observation: Ask if they see oppression and injustice in their district. Challenge

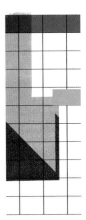

them to examine who is being advantaged. Discuss who has the seat of power and how it could be shared. The structures that have been built over time can be dismantled by passionate and convicted light-bearers. This is a prime time to come against the darkness of racism that has pervaded our culture for too long.

Q. **Some parents may feel they need to become better educated themselves about racial diversity and equity before coaching their kids. Is it possible for adults and children to learn alongside each other? If so, how?**

A. It is possible and preferable for adults and children to learn alongside each other!

In his first letter, the apostle John uses the phrase "dearly loved children" to address his audience. This reminds us that we are all children of God who have a lot of learning and growing yet to do.

I think it is incredibly inspiring for our children to see our journey of gaining knowledge in the area of racial diversity. Instead of taking pride in a supposed proficiency, the curiosity of children would be piqued to hear their parents admit a deficit of racial literacy. As there is no permanent antiracist status to achieve, we are all on a continuum of deconstructing myths and ignorance as we grow in wisdom.

"We are all children of God who have a lot of learning and growing yet to do."

Family reading time is a great way for parents and kids to dive into their own books and then share key points together. Do a bookshelf inventory of your titles and those of your children and reflect on the level of diversity present. As you talk about your day, share details from an insightful webinar you watched. Find movies with ratings that can be enjoyed at your child's level, keeping in mind that they often know more and are eager to go deeper than our own fragility may expect. Plan your next trip around civil rights museums that will give your family rich conversation points. Take your teen with you to hear antiracism authors who visit your city and reflect over dessert on what challenged you. Talk about the ethnic makeup of your neighborhood, school, church and city and research together how redlining, gentrification, disasters and historical events created a lack of diversity in certain communities. Discuss

what actions you can each take, such as speaking up at local school-board meetings, participating in protests, voting, advocating for underserved neighbors and joining community efforts led by people of color.

Q. **What are some age-appropriate ways to talk with early-grade children about racial and / or cultural differences? How do you see the conversation evolving or deepening in a healthy, God-honoring direction as kids get older?**

A. Conversations with early-grade children should start with the biblical foundation that God made all humankind in his image. Emphasize that God was delighted to intentionally fill creation with diversity. Reinforce to children that dehumanization steals from the beauty God made and is offensive to him. These core values should be repeated often.

As kids get older, they should be taught a fuller story of history: how the construct of race was established to place whiteness as supreme over every other skin color, and thus to perpetuate racism. Teach them that the sacrifice of Christ made one new body of believers who are called to be one, and who retain our distinctions as seen around the heavenly throne in Revelation. Do not whitewash our differences in gender, culture and economic status with a color-blind approach.

Families should be intentional to teach children their own ethnic story, including the successes and struggles of their ancestors. Teach this in view of a global context and remind kids that God always intended for every family on earth to be blessed, all the way back to the covenant he made with Abraham (see Genesis 11).

Be careful to not posture any ethnic group as "the needy." Teach that injustice crosses cultures and ethnic groups, and that we must constantly check our own biases and ask God to examine our own hearts. Train children to see differences as good and to grow diverse friendships with a heart to learn and connect rather than to disdain and demean.

As you raise young humans who will leave the nest one day, remember that values are passed down. Silence misses incredible opportunities to build a healthy racial foundation and leaves our children open for offensive teaching to infiltrate their vulnerable hearts. We must be proactive so that our descendants can learn from the stories we live out today. ▪

What's the Bigger Problem?

A practicing Christian's ranking of the greater problem—systemic racism or individual prejudice—correlates with many other ideas about inequity and race relations in our country. Generally, Christians who see individual prejudice as the greater harm—typically younger, rarely Black—are less likely to acknowledge disparities or to report personal motivation to address injustice.

■ % of each generation who sees racism as **SYSTEMIC**

▩ % of each generation who sees racism as INDIVIDUAL

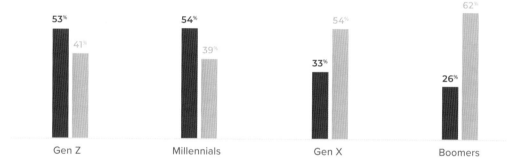

	Gen Z	Millennials	Gen X	Boomers
Systemic	53%	54%	33%	26%
Individual	41%	39%	54%	62%

■ % of each race group who sees racism as **SYSTEMIC**

▩ % of each race group who sees racism as INDIVIDUAL

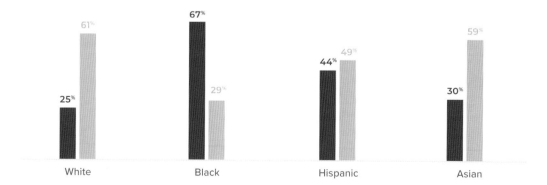

	White	Black	Hispanic	Asian
Systemic	25%	67%	44%	30%
Individual	61%	29%	49%	59%

12%: "I don't know"

33%:
"Racial discrimination that is historically built into our society and institutions"

55%:
"Individuals' own beliefs and prejudices that cause them to treat people of other races poorly"

■ Those who see racism as **SYSTEMIC** say...

▨ Those who see racism as INDIVIDUAL say...

"Our country definitely has a race problem"	"I am motivated to address racial injustice"	"Historically, the U.S. has been oppressive to minorities"

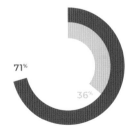

71%

36%

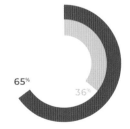

65%

36%

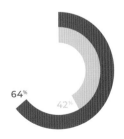

64%

42%

n=1,364 practicing Christians, July 19–August 5, 2019.

From the Focus Groups: Where History Meets Our Stories

"Racism was a part of America's founding. The original colonizers established segregation in order to control labor. Indentured servants were fading so it was replaced by slavery, which was cheaper. Legislation was created to make that possible. The white race was created when they and black people were deemed unable to marry by law. Racism is part of the American life. It provides cover for those who have the upper hand." *—Black congregant*

"I am hopeful that my grandchildren will be in a better place in this country. My children have done okay. I am committed to this country; it's mine, and I would like to see it better." *—Black congregant*

"Right now, I don't feel like I'm benefiting from other people being oppressed. But when I think about slavery, specifically the slavery that took place in our country, the systems that came out of that, there's still that gap that formed from that. ... I still think that we are somehow benefiting from the oppression that took place even back then when it was going on. I don't know for certain that we have broken away from all of that." *—White congregant*

"When I meet people of color, I have to acknowledge that people that look like me have done wrong to them and that changes things in a conversation." *—White congregant* ▮

continued from page 66

inequity as: lack of educational opportunities (37%); Black fathers leaving their families (33%); experiences of discrimination (31% ongoing, 29% in the past) and reliance on government assistance (26%).

So, what do Black practicing Christians believe—or perhaps personally experience?

By and large, they cite ongoing discrimination (67%) and say past discrimination continues to hold them back (49%). They also point to laws that have favored white people (38%) and say the public lacks trust in the potential of Black leaders (30%).

Black Christians are telling a clear, cohesive story, but white Christians don't appear to be listening. The louder narrative that Black Americans are only up against isolated hardship or moral failure can exacerbate racial bias. Myths about Black fathers or Black welfare recipients, though contradicted by experts and data, thrive on a lack of curiosity and empathy toward the lived experiences of generations of Black Americans.[26] Left unchallenged among white Christians, these mindsets present a significant barrier to addressing racism with compassion and clarity, especially in the Church.

Furthermore, this disconnect between the reality faced by Christians of color and the perceptions of white Christians complicates building diverse relationships, a solution that Christians of all races believe is worth pursuing. As the research shows, Christians of color admit having a difficult time connecting in multiracial contexts. These differences could well be part of the reason why; it's likely challenging to find trusting friendship with someone who views your racial group through the lens of pervasive misinformation and negative generalizations. Churches discipling white Christians or multiracial congregations have an opportunity, by explaining the facts of the lived experiences of people of color and by facilitating fair-minded relationships, to counter myths and confront this trend. ▪

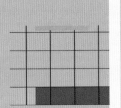

Splitting the Pews

Exploring the gaps in views of race, in graphic detail

A church's posture toward racial justice, or effectiveness in addressing it, may greatly depend on the races and ages of those in the congregation. This special section offers a brief visual overview of telling divides revealed in this study— some of which widened in real time as we continued our analysis.

Some questions were posed to respondents again in the summer of 2020, for comparison amid heightened racial tensions and demonstrations. The 2020 study does not have a large enough sample of practicing Christians to report on all of the same categories surveyed in the 2019 study. When looking at how faith intersects with race or generation in the following pages, we'll examine self-identified Christians for year-over-year comparisons.

Acknowledging the Present Problem

Do you think our country has a race problem?

% "definitely"

2019   ■ 2020

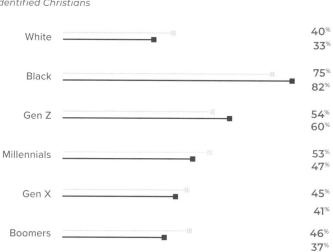

	2019	2020
All U.S. adults	49%	46%
Practicing Christians	46%	43%
Self-identified Christians	47%	43%

Among self-identified Christians

	2019	2020
White	40%	33%
Black	75%	82%
Gen Z	54%	60%
Millennials	53%	47%
Gen X	45%	41%
Boomers	46%	37%

n=2,289 U.S. adults, July 19–August 5, 2019.
n=1,525 U.S. adults, June 18–July 17, 2020.

1 in 5

of all practicing Christians says race is "not at all" a current problem in the U.S., as of summer 2020 (19%, up from 11% in 2019).

Acknowledging the Past Problem

"Historically, the United States has been oppressive to minorities"

% strongly + somewhat agree

‖ 2019　■ 2020

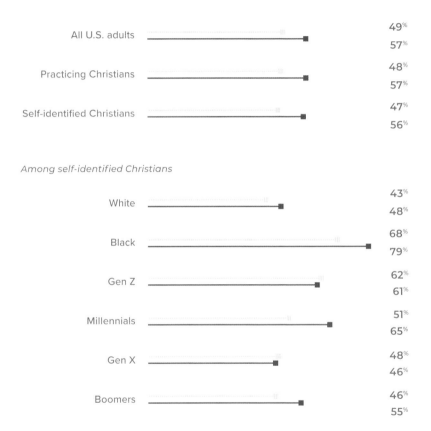

		2019	2020
All U.S. adults		49%	57%
Practicing Christians		48%	57%
Self-identified Christians		47%	56%

Among self-identified Christians

		2019	2020
White		43%	48%
Black		68%	79%
Gen Z		62%	61%
Millennials		51%	65%
Gen X		48%	46%
Boomers		46%	55%

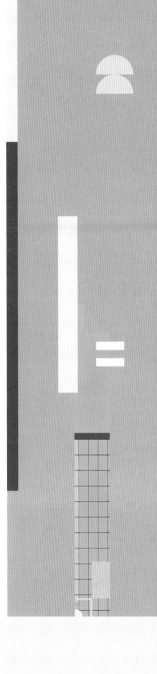

n=2,289 U.S. adults, July 19–August 5, 2019.
n=1,525 U.S. adults, June 18–July 17, 2020.

The percentage of Christians who are willing to acknowledge *past* injustice is growing. Those who strongly agree that, historically, the U.S. has oppressed minorities rose from 19% to 26% in one year.

Getting Involved

How motivated are you to address racial injustice?

% "very motivated" + "motivated"

▥ 2019 ■ 2020

	2019	2020
All U.S. adults	39%	35%
Practicing Christians	43%	41%
Self-identified Christians	39%	33%

Among self-identified Christians

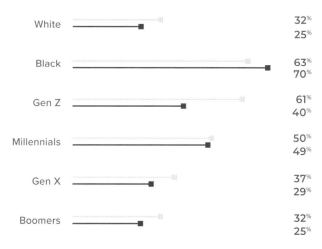

	2019	2020
White	32%	25%
Black	63%	70%
Gen Z	61%	40%
Millennials	50%	49%
Gen X	37%	29%
Boomers	32%	25%

n=2,289 U.S. adults, July 19–August 5, 2019.
n=1,525 U.S. adults, June 18–July 17, 2020.

46% of Black self-identified Christians report being "very" motivated to address racial injustice, up from 33% in 2019. White self-identified Christians who select this highest level of motivation declined (14% to 9%).

Ranking the Problem

Which of the following do you think is the bigger problem in the United States today?

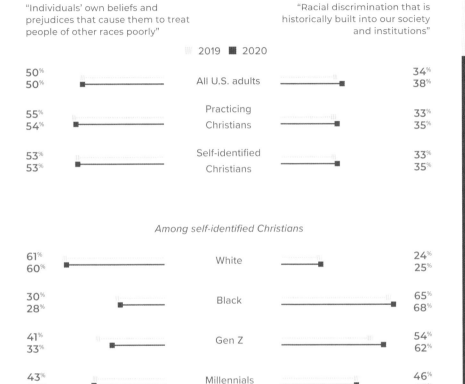

"Individuals' own beliefs and prejudices that cause them to treat people of other races poorly"

"Racial discrimination that is historically built into our society and institutions"

2019 ▪ 2020

	2019	2020		2019	2020
All U.S. adults	50%	50%		34%	38%
Practicing Christians	55%	54%		33%	35%
Self-identified Christians	53%	53%		33%	35%

Among self-identified Christians

	2019	2020		2019	2020
White	61%	60%		24%	25%
Black	30%	28%		65%	68%
Gen Z	41%	33%		54%	62%
Millennials	43%	44%		46%	46%
Gen X	57%	57%		30%	30%
Boomers	60%	58%		27%	26%

n=2,289 U.S. adults, July 19–August 5, 2019.
n=1,525 U.S. adults, June 18–July 17, 2020.

White and Black self-identified Christians' views are essentially flipped when it comes to identifying roots of racism.

See page 70 for more on how this fundamental question connects with other gaps in opinion.

Identifying Reasons for Inequality

Based on statistics, on average Black people have lower quality jobs, housing and income than white people. Why do you think this is?

■ White practicing Christians   ■ Black practicing Christians

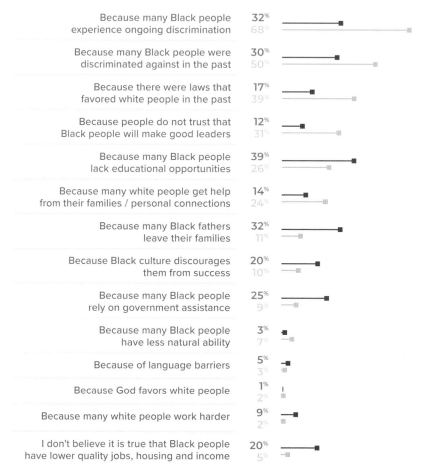

Reason	White	Black
Because many Black people experience ongoing discrimination	32%	68%
Because many Black people were discriminated against in the past	30%	50%
Because there were laws that favored white people in the past	17%	39%
Because people do not trust that Black people will make good leaders	12%	31%
Because many Black people lack educational opportunities	39%	26%
Because many white people get help from their families / personal connections	14%	24%
Because many Black fathers leave their families	32%	11%
Because Black culture discourages them from success	20%	10%
Because many Black people rely on government assistance	25%	9%
Because many Black people have less natural ability	3%	7%
Because of language barriers	5%	3%
Because God favors white people	1%	2%
Because many white people work harder	9%	2%
I don't believe it is true that Black people have lower quality jobs, housing and income	20%	5%

n=978 U.S. practicing Christians, July 19–August 5, 2019.

2x Black practicing Christians are more than twice as likely as white practicing Christians to attribute racial inequities to ongoing discrimination of their community. White practicing Christians are far more likely to deny inequities, or to ascribe them to personal or cultural shortcomings among Black people.

4. Privilege & Disadvantage:

Understanding how race impacts our lives

Some Christians may rarely observe the nuances of racial diversity because they rarely observe their own racial experience in the first place.

Thus far in this report, we've seen that white practicing Christians are generally hesitant to think about their own race, hesitant to say racial minorities face discrimination—and, likewise, they are hesitant to say that being white gives them a boost.

Meanwhile, Black practicing Christians are the most likely racial group to acknowledge a disadvantage due to their race. In fact, the proportion of Black practicing Christians who say being Black has hurt their ability to get ahead (39%) roughly equals that of white practicing Christians who perceive their race has helped them. Though Hispanic practicing Christians are the most likely minority to report some advantage, 28 percent still acknowledge some obstacles due to their racial identity. For the most part, Asian practicing Christians have no strong feeling on the topic; 51 percent say being Asian has neither hurt nor helped them in life.

White practicing Christians are most likely to resist evidence that being white provides them societal benefits. They may feel that the nuances of their own choices and life stories matter more than any broader racial advantage (for instance, the fact that a white-sounding name on a resume increases chances of being hired).[27]

In focus groups, primary arguments against the idea that white people have inherent advantages echo a meritocracy or some form of the "American Dream" narrative: "If you work hard, you'll be successful," or "I had to work hard, and that's why I've been successful." By the same token, we see that white survey respondents who dismiss the idea that they've been given a leg up because they are white are often more inclined to see individual rather than institutional forms of racial discrimination as most damaging. In other words, white respondents who deny their own privilege voice less empathy for the struggles of other racial groups. Meanwhile, white practicing Christians who regard systemic racial injustice as the larger issue are far more likely to say being white has helped them.

More than one-third of white practicing Christians (36%) says their race has given them advantages. Only 5 percent say that being white negatively impacts their ability to get ahead. The next lowest figure on this side of the scale is with Asian Christians, where 21 percent say that being Asian hurts them at least a little bit.

Some white Christians may fear that admitting an inherent advantage negates their accomplishments. Theologically, church leaders have an opportunity to help congregants navigate the realities of prejudice and privilege,

Overall, has the following helped or hurt your ability to get ahead?

Practicing Christians

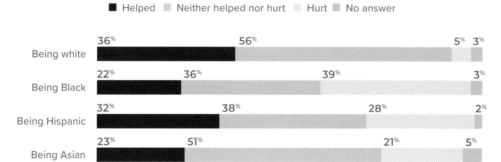

n=1,364 practicing Christians, July 19–August 5, 2019.
Respondents were only asked to answer about the race with which they identify.

Overall, has being white helped or hurt your ability to get ahead?

White practicing Christians by view of racism

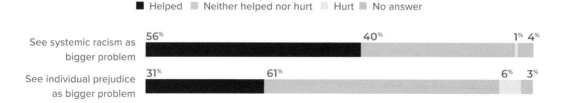

n=720 white practicing Christians, July 19–August 5, 2019.

justice and compassion. Practically, they also have an opportunity to model or encourage acknowledgement of racial privilege and to lift up or create opportunity for those with less social capital or privilege.

As in other points of this study, among white practicing Christians, younger generations are more likely to say being white gives them some ability to get ahead. One in four white practicing Christian Millennials (25%) says their race has helped them "a lot," and though the white practicing Christian Gen Z segment is too small to report on here, the early pattern in their responses suggests they strongly feel the same. Gen X and Boomers are largely neutral on whether this advantage exists, even though their generation benefited from government programs, legal segregation and widespread discrimination in the private sector.[28]

Though the term "white privilege" is now relatively mainstream, it provokes mixed feelings in respondents. White practicing Christians feel angry, judged or sad, with nearly one-third, respectively, selecting these emotions.

From the Focus Groups: Wrestling with White Privilege

"I think [white privilege] is a word thrown around quite a lot. I think it is racist. It does not equally apply to everyone. Some people are taller, and they can reach the top shelf. But to blanket an entire race like that? That is discrimination. I also think there is a lot of guilt around it. You are condemning people for a crime they did not commit."—*White congregant*

"[All my white friends] feel like they are becoming the minority. They feel like they are economically disempowered, they can't even buy homes or can't go to schools where whites are the majority. I am exhausted for them."—*Asian congregant*

"It's willful ignorance. When you're privileged, you don't want to give it up. You don't want to share it, so it's easier to ignore it and keep things the way they are. Basically, negotiating this stuff is exhausting. So, I don't want [to]. I'm not interested. I pray that they get it, but in the meantime, I'm going to live my best life."—*Black congregant*

Overall, has being white helped or hurt your ability to get ahead?
White practicing Christians by generation

■ Helped ▓ Neither helped nor hurt ░ Hurt ▒ No answer

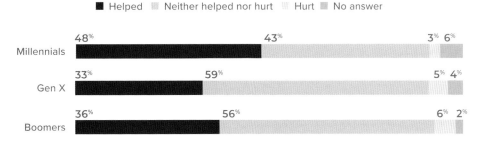

	Helped	Neither helped nor hurt	Hurt	No answer
Millennials	48%	43%	3%	6%
Gen X	33%	59%	5%	4%
Boomers	36%	56%	6%	2%

n=720 white practicing Christians, July 19–August 5, 2019.
White practicing Christian samples among Gen Z and Elders are too small to be shown.

In focus groups, some white adults feel confused or upset about "reverse racism" when white privilege is brought up. Meanwhile, Black and Hispanic Christians also experience anger over white privilege, though this feeling is more rooted in fear, powerlessness or frustration that such injustice or unfairness exists.

Some feel judged, defensive or even angry about "reverse racism" when the concept of "white privilege" is brought up.

Overall, most white participants are not ready or willing to admit if they have received greater opportunity because of the color of their skin. Interestingly, this is the case even if they are willing to admit the inverse, that Black, Hispanic or Asian people are singled out in a negative way because of their racial identity. ■

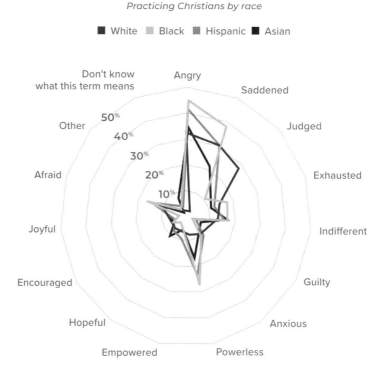

Emotions About "White Privilege"
Practicing Christians by race

■ White ▦ Black ▦ Hispanic ■ Asian

n=1,364 practicing Christians, July 19–August 5, 2019.

by Chad Brennan

DIRECTOR OF RENEW PARTNERSHIPS

A Problematic or Essential Concept?

As the data and comments above show, the topic of "white privilege" often sparks a wide range of emotions and responses. With our work and research, we find that there is a great deal of confusion about the concept. I hope the following Q&A can help to clarify a few key areas.

What is white privilege and how do we know it exists?

White privilege refers to the special advantages that white people in the U.S. receive because of their race. There is an enormous amount of research that confirms the existence of white privilege. Several examples were shared earlier in this report (see page 55). For additional examples, I recommend the five-minute video "Systemic Racism Explained" and the 17-minute video "Race in America."[29]

How was white privilege created?

Since the earliest days of European colonization, many white people have intentionally created economic, political, education, and religious systems that advantaged themselves and disadvantaged people of color. Over time, white colonists created a racial hierarchy with white people at the top and Black people at the bottom. Other people of color (Indigenous, Hispanic / Latino, Asian, etc.) typically fall somewhere between the two extremes. The white privilege that exists in the U.S. today was created through the collective actions of millions of people over hundreds of years. A few examples include restricting citizenship to white people, racially segregating schools and limiting voting opportunities for people of color.

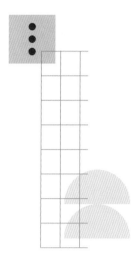

How does inaction sustain white privilege?

Those of us who are white were born into a society that is structured to give us special privileges. The only thing we need to do to keep receiving those privileges is not address them. One of the most common ways that white people consciously or unconsciously help to perpetuate white privilege is through inaction and apathy toward issues of racial justice.

How does "not seeing" past or present racial injustice sustain white privilege?

Social research has shown that people tend to reject information that does not align with their understanding of reality or which would require them to change their behavior in ways that they do not want to change. That tendency is known as "motivated reasoning." Motivated reasoning helps to explain why white people are the most inclined to disagree with statements like, "Historically, the United States has been oppressive to minorities" (see page 54). Agreeing with that statement may challenge their view of themselves and our society, as well as cause them to feel a sense of responsibility to address racial injustice. Instead, they choose to reject that reality.

Does white privilege exist in Christian organizations?

Unfortunately, white privilege continues to be a powerful reality both in our society and in many Christian organizations. Throughout U.S. history, many Christians and Christian organizations have supported racial injustice and white privilege rather than standing against it. Over the last 15 years, my organization has studied racial dynamics in Christian organizations across the U.S. We find that white privilege and white normativity continue to have a powerful influence in predominantly white Christian organizations. Dr. Korie Edwards provides a helpful explanation of those realities in the book *The Elusive Dream*.[30]

Why are efforts to address white privilege often viewed as "unfair treatment?"

When those of us who are white are used to receiving special advantages, losing them can be a difficult and disorienting process. Efforts to eliminate white privilege are often viewed as "unfair treatment" or "reverse racism" by white people. They do not recognize that white privilege is inherently unfair because it is giving one group special advantages at the expense of other groups. Therefore, working toward eliminating white privilege is providing justice for people of color, not taking justice away from white people.

Why is there often a "sacrifice ceiling" for support for racial justice efforts?

Measuring support for racial justice efforts is difficult. If you ask, "Do you support efforts to work toward racial justice in our society and your organization?" a large percentage of people of all races typically says yes. However, the true level of our support becomes apparent when we are in situations where our support requires personal sacrifice. Many white people withdraw their support or push back on efforts when it requires them to give up their favored status or resources. ▨

Brittany Wade

FOUNDER OF WILDFIRE RESEARCH;
RESEARCH DESIGN / ANALYSIS,
INTERVIEWER

Lessons from Focus Groups:
How Unacknowledged White Normativity
Harms the Church

Stop for a moment and consider: What does it mean to be a part of your race? What is your racial culture?

I ask those questions in trainings I facilitate. When I ask Black participants, "What does it mean to be Black?" the responses carry sentiments of "creativity, courage, resilience." When I ask Asian participants, "What does it mean to be Asian?" they include phrases such as "family, caretaking and good food." When white participants respond, I hear about "not worrying about race, having everything made for you, not being uncomfortable." (My favorite response? "Neil Diamond.")

White culture is seen only in contrast to what it is to be "other." But people of color have a level of race-consciousness that is developed in response to an incident or sudden realization that something about them is not "normal." This can happen in a number of different ways—often in regular, everyday situations where people of color realize the things they think, know, say or do are not considered normal. This feeling, initially noticed at a young age, is consistently reaffirmed through life experiences for people of color.

As stated at the beginning of this chapter, "we've seen that white practicing Christians are hesitant to think about their own race, hesitant to say racial minorities face discrimination—and, likewise, they are hesitant to say that being white gives them a boost." As I reviewed and analyzed focus groups for this research, their conversations expanded upon the notion that white respondents are less race-conscious—meaning they less often understand how their race factors into decisions, thoughts, cultural norms and societal structures. The impact of this lack of understanding—which I'd attribute to willful ignorance—is white normativity.

There is an unintentional but harmful view that what white people think is normal and should be seen as such by everyone else. Anything other than this normal is deemed ethnic, foreign, suspect or less-than, rather than appreciated as what it is: someone else's normal. This white normativity has been held over people of color in ways that result in assimilation into what is seen as the "correct" majority culture. The impact is a foregoing of identity and dignity by people of color to fit in and be seen.

The survey shows that Black practicing Christians are the most likely racial category to sense a disadvantage due to their race, and this was reflected in our focus groups. Here's how one participant, a Black respondent at a majority white multiracial church, puts it:

"I feel like [this church] is a multicolored service, but it is not a multicultural church. ... We're not multicultural, because, ultimately, I feel like you don't see me and, if you don't see, then how can you serve [me], and how can I be ministered to here if you don't even acknowledge that I'm here or my specific needs or my specific struggles? A lot of people come here because they're struggling with something. I need answers. They're looking for answers from God, from somewhere, and you are representatives of God, but you're ignoring my wounds. Honestly, that's a moment of struggle for me pretty constantly [whether to leave the church]. Am I supposed to be here if I'm not really here?"

When Christians of color realize that white normativity is accepted and, at times, expected, a wrestling happens—between whether to stay in a place where they feel unseen, or whether to assimilate into the culture so that they can be seen.

And here is an example from a Hispanic participant who speaks to how being bilingual is seen as less-than or foreign:

"I have experienced racism. Sometimes, it isn't your skin or where you work, it's how you communicate to others. Sometimes, I wish I didn't have an accent, so that I could be normal and blend into the community. If you are Indian and have that accent, people look at you differently. Same with Spanish. But when you don't have the accent, that's good."

This value of white normativity is translated for people of color as, "Change who you are to fit in so that you all can be seen as better—and then accepted."

White normativity starts to turn into white supremacy when a sense of dominion over others enters into how white people talk, interact and disciple others. In his book *White Lies,* pastor Daniel Hill talks about white supremacy this way: Evil principalities divide and distort the image of God, based on a set of lies that

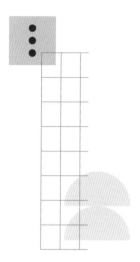

assign superiority to whiteness and inferiority to Blackness, and measure all human value based on perceived proximity to the two poles.[31]

In the Christian Church, this measure of superiority to inferiority is seen by some people of color, but there is a cultural understanding to leave it unacknowledged. To acknowledge and talk about this would make people—white people in particular—uncomfortable and would disturb the power structure.

As a Black focus group participant says, "The most segregated day of the week is Sunday. Because we do not understand each other's story. Why should we rock the boat? We don't want to hurt anyone's feelings. If we start dealing with race, we can easily start running people off."

Avoiding these conversations does not create a sense of unity or solidarity on the topic of race and diversity; on the contrary, it actually creates a false sense of peace. As seen in chapter one, it is creating an environment that forces some people of color to give up part of their racial identity to fit in, even at church. This hinders the potential to build relationships, grow the church and move into power-sharing leadership. It means that we are only telling one side of the story, communicating it as if it is the whole story.

> "Avoiding these conversations does not create a sense of unity or solidarity on the topic of race and diversity; on the contrary, it actually creates a false sense of peace."

One question we asked focus group participants is, "What is the top priority for the Church right now?" A majority of participants rates "being relevant to the current culture" as the top priority for Christians today. They also identify "equity and inclusion" as a top priority for culture today. I read that and wonder: By not addressing equity and inclusion, are we not actively ignoring a key part of cultural relevance? It harms the Church's relevance if we don't educate, have open dialogue and then move to action for racial justice.

The Church is meant to be a place of love, inclusion and advocacy for racial justice. If we are limiting ourselves to the expression of one cultural identity, experience and reflection of who God is, we are not just wounding people of color—we are wounding *all* of God's people. We must lean into conversation and action and be open to change within our churches in order to dismantle the "normal." Let's not continue to build upon old foundations but create new ones that are an example to the world. ▥

5. Us & Them:

How emotions & scripture factor into views of immigrants

Today, well over 40 million U.S. residents were born in another nation.[32] Some came for the promise of a better life and economic opportunity. Some to escape war, famine or oppression. It's painful to fathom that some were—and some still are—brought to the nation without their consent. Whatever the reason, the majority of U.S. adults (75%), including practicing Christians (83%), agrees: "Historically, the U.S. has been a nation of immigrants." Indeed, one in four practicing Christians is either an immigrant themselves or the child of one.

But even agreement on this fact obscures a variety of present-day views on the subject of immigration. Today in the U.S., conversations about immigration typically focus on migrants crossing the U.S.-Mexican border or refugees from Muslim-majority nations—as well as conflicting political opinions about their presence. At the time of this writing, President Joe Biden has recommitted to a broad effort to reverse immigration policies from President Donald Trump's administration.[33] How churches respond to immigration growth will be crucial in the near future, especially for congregations being intentional about becoming more diverse or pursuing justice for the marginalized.

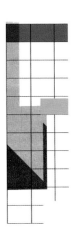

The emotions surrounding this topic are somewhat more complex than simple ethnoreligious or race-based animus against immigrant groups. We asked U.S. adults what terms or emotions they associate with "undocumented immigrants," specifically. Mostly, they feel "saddened" (33%), "angry" (26%) and "powerless" (21%) when they hear the phrase, sentiments that are shared by practicing Christians (36% saddened, 27% angry, 20% powerless).

By race, we see a spike in anger among white practicing Christians (31%). Hispanic practicing Christians, often a subject of these conversations, are most likely to feel "judged" (20%). Beyond sadness (37%), Asian practicing Christians select a range of emotions, but do not as commonly experience the sense of guilt or judgment that afflicts their Hispanic peers. Black Christians report feeling "indifferent" (20%) more often than other groups, perhaps indicating the need for additional engagement in these conversations.

Focus group responses expand on these reported emotions—or, perhaps, illustrate the difference between what an individual might state privately in an online survey and overtly in an in-person discussion. For instance, when the word "angry" was chosen, some Christians (white ones especially) add

Emotions About "Undocumented Immigrants"

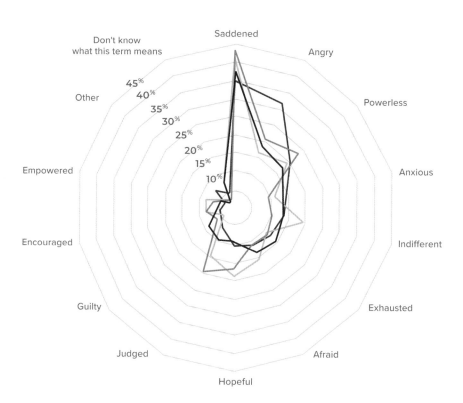

n=1,364 U.S. practicing Christians, July 19–August 5, 2019.

that their anger is a result of seeing and learning how undocumented immigrants are treated, not hostility *toward* immigrants.

Hispanic practicing Christians are likely to associate the term "undocumented immigrants" with feeling "saddened" and "judged."

Focus group participants differ widely, however, in their support of legal protections and solutions for immigrants. White and Asian Christians are more likely to be proponents of what they deem a "right way" to immigrate (that is, legal paths including getting a visa or applying for citizenship, rather than working and living in the U.S. while undocumented), while Black and Hispanic Christians are more likely to say immigrants should be loved and cared for, no matter their context, means of entry or place on the path to citizenship.

The survey results echo this divide over policy. Two in three practicing Christians agree we should have laws that protect immigrants from being treated unfairly (29% strongly agree, 19% agree, 17% somewhat agree). This is in line with the number in the general population in favor of these protections (31% strongly agree, 18% agree, 16% somewhat agree), and is driven by strong support from Black and Hispanic practicing Christians. White practicing Christians, however, are less than half as likely as Christians of color to strongly support laws protecting immigrants (23%).

Seeing this array of emotions and views by race—taken together with the reality that there

From the Focus Groups: Responses to Immigrants

"I'm sad about the whole situation. I don't see how anyone can justify this. Sure, they are here illegally, but there has to be a pathway to citizenship. You see the children; it's inhumane. They treated us like that. It's just a sad situation. To think people believe they have the power to do that. I know people who stock up food on the weekends because they know ICE is patrolling."—*Black congregant*

"It makes me angry because they are treated like a subpar human being. There is some malice associated with that situation, when usually that is a person who is trying to better their life. I am sure there is some grey to it, but in general I am tired of the political rhetoric about it."—*White congregant*

"I am not sure which way is better: coming here and getting a career, or staying back home and not being discriminated against? There I will be poor, but I will be with my family. Here I will work one or two jobs, be stressed and not be with my family."—*Hispanic congregant*

"I feel like our nation is in the midst of a real struggle, especially when you're talking about immigrant populations and Jesus saying 'bring a stranger in.' I think the things that we're facing are historic in nature. And unless we peel back and look at the genesis of that, we're going to end up falling short, as the church. … When Christ judges us, what is he going to look at? Did we do the right thing? Did we take care of the widow, the orphan, the foreigner?"—*Black congregant*

"There is ongoing rhetoric even now—the hateful rhetoric about immigrants that gets said—but then there is silence in the church because they want to be politically neutral. You can be politically neutral and still care about the body of Christ. … Whether it is [because of] fear or indifference, whatever it is, we have allowed the world to speak up first and what it has shown differently is more, sadly, hatred and bigotry from a Christian point of view."—*White congregant* ▮

is not, in fact, widespread buy-in to the idea that immigrants pose an economic threat to U.S. citizens, as shown above—it's no wonder immigration is among the minefields of the political landscape.

Turning to Scripture

Racial justice in the Church, including care for immigrants, at some point becomes a scriptural issue—for people of all colors and for congregations of all contexts.

"We should have laws that protect immigrants from being treated unfairly"

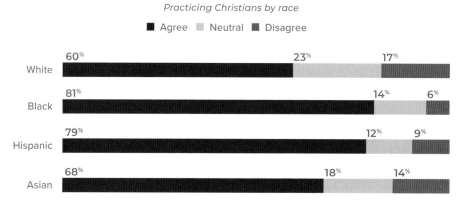

Practicing Christians by race

■ Agree   ▨ Neutral   ▩ Disagree

	Agree	Neutral	Disagree
White	60%	23%	17%
Black	81%	14%	6%
Hispanic	79%	12%	9%
Asian	68%	18%	14%

n=1,364 practicing Christians, July 19–August 5, 2019.

"Immigrants coming into the U.S. are taking too many jobs from U.S. citizens"

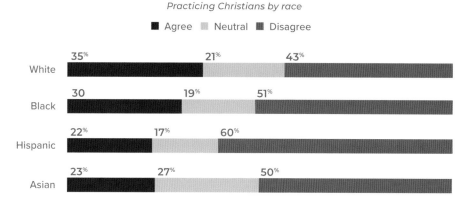

Practicing Christians by race

■ Agree   ▨ Neutral   ▩ Disagree

	Agree	Neutral	Disagree
White	35%	21%	43%
Black	30	19%	51%
Hispanic	22%	17%	60%
Asian	23%	27%	50%

n=1,364 practicing Christians, July 19–August 5, 2019.

Barna presented survey respondents with Bible passages and interpretations to gauge if they see certain verses as examples of how to relate to marginalized groups. They were first asked how often the Bible should be used to determine what is right or wrong; two-thirds of practicing Christians say "always," and the other one-third says "sometimes." So, we know this is a group who feels strongly that scripture should help direct how they live. Yet participants' capacity to apply scripture to today's context varies greatly.

Though Barna surveyed about multiple passages and principles, we'll illustrate the trend of our findings through one example—related to immigration, a topic that, as we've just covered, prompts strong feelings in Christians.

On the whole, practicing Christians agree, either strongly or somewhat, with this summary: In the system of laws that God gave the Israelites to follow, there were laws that protected foreigners from being treated unjustly. Therefore, it is good to have laws that protect foreigners from being treated unjustly.

A small proportion is unsure, and only a very small proportion disagrees. Black practicing Christians lead all minorities in being more likely than white practicing Christians to strongly agree with this statement. This is a consistent pattern that emerges for all texts in this exercise: Based on how the questions were framed, white Christians are less likely than Black and Hispanic Christians to resonate with the scripture interpretations provided. Asian Christians fall somewhere in between, sometimes connecting with the suggested applications, and other times not.

From the Focus Groups: Connections Between Scripture & Justice

"I am not guilty for the crimes of my father, but if there is something I can do to remedy it, then I should. You should lessen the burden. You can still show compassion, but there is no obligation to do so. Well, maybe there is, but it depends on the crime. If my father stole from someone's inheritance, for example, and I benefited from that I should pay it back. But, how could you measure that? How far back do you go?"—*White congregant*

"I went up to [Nehemiah 1:4] and it says, 'He sat down and wept. In fact, for days, I mourned, fasted and prayed to the God of heaven.' So, he's empathizing and sympathizing with these people. It matters to him. I think that is important too. I used to do announcements at our church, and it was after one of the shootings. I couldn't get up there and do the announcements, looking into the crowd. I just started crying because I know these people, and I can't just get up here joyfully and say my announcements without saying I love you all, and you are worthy, and I'm sorry for what has happened. Not because I did it, but there are injustices and I'm sorry for that, because that stinks. And you are made in the image of God, and we are both equal. I'm not higher than you, you're not higher than me, so I'm sorry. Just being able to sit. Even the scriptures say, 'Weep with those who weep; rejoice with those who rejoice.'"—*White congregant*

"I believe the Bible is the truth, and God's truth. In the context of understanding the Bible historically, but also asking the Holy Spirit to help us understand it spiritually. Not just asking what the verses are talking about, but also praying over them to know what I should learn from it." —*Asian congregant*

"I believe that a holistic gospel is one that addresses individual salvation and spiritual transformation, that it also includes development, not just simply giving [a fish in an] act of mercy to someone but teaching them to fish. But then if they can't get access to the lake because there's a fence around it, cutting a hole in the fence, which is the social justice piece—biblical justice—so they have access to what God gave them. I look at all policies that way."
—*White congregant*

Subsequently, we asked a similar version of the above question, but this time, we also referenced a Bible verse that supported the statement:

"Do not take advantage of a hired worker who is poor and needy, whether that worker is a fellow Israelite or a foreigner residing in one of your towns" (Deuteronomy 24:14).

Interestingly, six out of 10 practicing Christians who previously either disagreed or were neutral as to whether the U.S. should have laws that protect immigrants from unfair treatment (61%) agreed at least somewhat with the second version of the question that referenced the related verse.

"In the system of laws that God gave the Israelites to follow, there were laws that protected foreigners from being treated unjustly. Therefore, it is good to have laws that protect foreigners from being treated unjustly."

Practicing Christians by race

■ Strongly agree   ■ Agree   ■ Not sure   ■ Disagree   ■ Strongly disagree

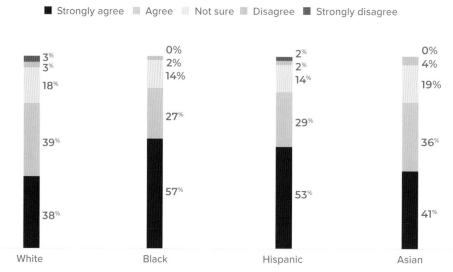

n=1,364 practicing Christians, July 19–August 5, 2019.

What to make of this? Realistically, this doesn't necessarily mean a scripture reference in a survey *changed* minds. And theoretical application is not the same as actual application. However, this experiment demonstrates the power of teaching scripture with applications to present-day justice. At least, it trains Christians to wrestle with a passage or idea. At most, it directly informs changes in thought and action.

Within and beyond this one exercise, our research showed Christians who are more aware of a range of injustices today connect these issues to biblical teaching. In our focus groups, Christians of *all* races who express strong understanding of systemic racism or who engage in lament and corporate repentance tend to also articulate scripturally based arguments for racial justice or caring for immigrants. This biblical literacy almost always coincides with accounts of receiving frequent and deep teaching from the pulpit about issues of justice, underscoring pastors' responsibility to shepherd their congregations through tough subjects.

Teaching that scripture applies to our present-day efforts to pursue justice and mercy is a key step in Christian discipleship.

It's possible these respondents are among the one-third (35%) who want the Church to teach about how the Bible encourages special kindness to marginalized groups (see page 107). They've seen the power of such "lightbulb moments." Not all biblically literate Christians understand and are concerned about justice issues— but those Christians who most strongly advocate for justice commonly exhibit deep and rich biblical knowledge.

The need for scriptural discipleship concerning race and justice is reflected in this project's many interviews with church and academic leaders who have been engaged in racial reconciliation and justice efforts for many years. Though they caution that simply *knowing* a verse is not enough to manifest change, they also note seeing progress when Christians begin to connect the teaching of both Old and New Testaments to how God calls us to live in society and toward those who experience discrimination, including immigrants.

Overall, our online survey, our focus groups and our expert interviewees issue a clarion call: Teaching that scripture applies to our present-day efforts to pursue justice and mercy doesn't just help Christians navigate current social issues, it is a key step in Christian discipleship.

Eliezer Bonilla, Jr.

NATIONAL HISPANIC MILLENNIAL
DIRECTOR FOR THE NATIONAL HISPANIC
CHRISTIAN LEADERSHIP CONFERENCE;
ASSOCIATE PASTOR AT ABUNDANT LIFE
CHURCH OF GOD

Q&A

The Value of the Immigrant Church in the U.S.

Q. A multiracial worship environment can, perhaps counterintuitively, amplify existing prejudices and tensions. Have you observed this dynamic? How does your leadership team navigate the challenges of ministering to many different demographics?

A. Absolutely. For context, a vast majority of our congregation is Hispanic-Latino, but just because we're all Latinos doesn't mean that we all share the same culture or speak the same languages. Our worship has to be bilingual, and the music choice can be polarizing at times.

We integrated our worship back in 2003, so we've learned a lot over those two decades. We've noticed that whenever we decide to jump cultures, not just languages, there can be a disconnect. Stylistically, whether it's in English or in Spanish, a Hillsong song won't be a Latino song because it won't dive into a Latino cultural style. So, in a bilingual service, we choose one or two songs which are culturally more immigrant-leaning.

Newcomers may be a bit lost the first time, because it breaks the flow that they're used to in a one-culture church. But they get used to it, and the engaged attitude of the worship leader and the leadership in the church really helps.

Q. How do you see the national conversation surrounding racial justice unfolding in your local and ministry context?

A. We're open and vocal about our stances on justice and equality. We speak about it in the pulpit with microphone in hand.

We choose to remain conscious of justice issues every week, not just when they're in the media. We believe that the Spirit can speak into all of these things, no matter what we're talking about on that day.

Now, we have different political groups in our church, ranging from uber-conservative to very blue and Democratic. So, talking politics can cause a lot of polarization. We choose not to talk politics; we choose to talk thematically and ideologically. We will talk from a biblical lens.

We stay anchored in the Word and we don't shy away from what the Word has to say, even if it illuminates that your political affiliation might not have it all correct. That's what we've committed to.

Q. Do you see any generational differences as well when it comes to how people are talking about justice, race, diversity and those related issues?

A. Absolutely. Especially with parents who immigrated as adults, it's hard for them to assimilate into the greater American culture, especially in South Texas, where we have a large immigrant population. You can go your entire life in San Antonio without learning English and you'll be fine.

But then, their kids grow up in this culture and they learn the language quickly, they assimilate quickly. Their older parents face a cultural gap.

So, in these conversations about politics and justice and equality, that chasm of understanding broadens. The generations are looking through different cultural lenses.

Q. What unique gifts, experiences or hard-won lessons does the immigrant Church bring to the American Church?

A. From the Latino perspective, we have a depth of spirituality that has been lost in the American Church. Culturally, we have deep spiritual roots, both traditional Catholicism and the boom in Protestantism and Spirit-led movements.

I think that the North American Church is missing the spiritual component of these conversations on peacemaking and unity. They've been politicized. But the Latino immigrant is not necessarily carrying the baggage of North America. So, there's a sense of almost innocence and purity when it comes to

Latino spirituality within the United States. It's very grateful, very humble, very family-centric. The immigrant Church is a breath of fresh air.

Now, speaking on immigrants that come from the majority world—immigrants from Asia and Africa—the Eastern perspective on spirituality does not separate secular and spiritual. These immigrants often allow their spirituality to live through the totality of their lives, unlike the American Church, where the separation of church and state is institutionalized.

> "[Latino spirituality] is very grateful, very humble, very family-centric. The immigrant Church is a breath of fresh air."

That understanding, that we're ultimately spiritual beings with a physical body that will one day perish, the understanding that our spirituality is important all the time—I think that if we allow that portion of the immigrant Church to teach us that reality, we'll be better for it. ■

Rev. Dr. Alexia Salvatierra

CO-AUTHOR OF *FAITH-ROOTED ORGANIZING*

One in Christ in a Tribal Society

We're in an extraordinarily tribal moment in our society. We're all tribed up. You could blame [President Trump]. You could blame the media. You could blame Facebook. And really, all of these factors harden tribal lines, which are ancient and almost primordial. We all feel it. The idea of standing up to our own fills us with fear, because the tribe is where we belong, where we are safe. There are real penalties when we transgress our tribe, and I think it's incredibly important to recognize, rather than belittle, people's fears.

What does it mean to be one in Christ? It means we have Spirit-empowered courage to stand against our tribe when necessary for the sake of the gospel. The gospel came into a world that was all tribed up. The coming of the Holy Spirit empowered and enabled people across hardened tribal lines to create a new community that transcends Jew, Gentile, male, female, slave and free.

I think we're in a time right now, though, when Christians need to relearn how to be in community with one another across tribal lines. Through my more than 40 years of community organizing, I've become convinced that words and ideas can only get us so far. We all like the *idea* of being one in Christ. But *incarnating* oneness in Christ means we invest ourselves in relationships that pull us toward him and each other and transform us in the process.

Some years ago, I was director of Clergy and Laity United for Economic Justice of California and was working with many of the large evangelical churches in Orange County on immigration reform. The gap in values and perspectives then was similar to now: very hot, very divided, high emotions all around.

We started by bringing pastors together, 14 Anglo and 14 Hispanic immigrant pastors, to pray and listen. The Hispanic pastors were brave enough to share what was happening in their congregations. They shared how an ineffective, illogical and unjust immigration system was tearing families apart and destroying young people's dreams.

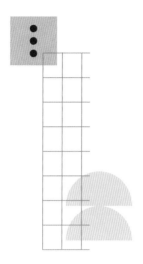

The white pastors were also brave. They shared about their fears related to the ministry impact of standing with immigrants. One leader told about his experience preaching on immigration justice and 200 families leaving his church the next week.

Then Dr. Juan Martinez, who was at Fuller Theological Seminary at the time, stood and said, "If we're dominated by fear, who are we? Are we or aren't we people who will carry the cross?"

Nobody breathed for a long moment, then we all got down to the business of wisely and creatively figuring out non-suicidal ways to activate white congregations. Those Anglo pastors were ready to carry the cross, but we all wanted to be sure any offense they suffered was the offense of Christ rather than of foolishness.

> "Those Anglo pastors were ready to carry the cross, but we all wanted to be sure any offense they suffered was the offense of Christ rather than of foolishness."

We ultimately designed a program for lay leaders in white and Hispanic congregations to partner with one another in mission. There was a children's detention center in Fullerton at the time, and so we started a prison ministry for the kids wherein these lay leaders came together to offer vacation Bible school, cooking classes, soccer games and other activities.

Our hope was that, over time, these lay leaders would build incarnational, transformative relationships. We planned for it to be a long, slow process.

But what actually happened is that one of the white megachurch board members was paired with a Hispanic leader doing kids' ministry at the detention center and, after just a few weeks, storms into the senior pastor's office and says, "The board has to talk about this. We have to talk about this as a church. This is not politics, it's people! Children are suffering!"

The wonderful thing about evangelicals is that, when push comes to shove, we can be fearless when the Spirit moves. If we know something is of God, we don't care who we have to face down.

This and other experiences fill me with hope, even in this dark moment. At our best, the Church thinks long term. I remind my students that we need both revolutionary *im*patience—to keep us in pursuit of God's justice—and revolutionary *patience*, to keep us trusting in the God of miracles, whose Spirit unites us as one in Christ. ▧

Adapted from an interview with Chad Brennan. Used by permission

6. Sunday & Every Day:

Opportunities for the Church to work toward solutions

As the Church determines how to move forward, it has yet to reach common ground on views of racial justice—or on a general desire to be a part of it. The data suggest that Christians are actually doubling down on these divides. Moving the Christian community beyond diversity is not getting any easier.

When we asked, "How motivated are you to address racial injustice in our society?" we see numbers moving—toward being *less* motivated.[34] In 2019, one in five U.S. adults was "unmotivated" (11%) or "not at all motivated" (9%); in the summer of 2020, after the protests following the murder of George Floyd, that percentage increased to 28 percent (12% "unmotivated," 16% "not at all motivated"). Meanwhile, the number of those who are "somewhat motivated" shrank and the number of those who are motivated held fairly steady, indicating some of those who might have previously been on the fence about addressing racial injustice have become more firmly opposed to engaging.

In one year, there was a 13-percentage-point increase overall in Christians who are unmotivated to address racial injustice.

For practicing Christians, the number of those who were unmotivated in 2019 (9% "unmotivated," 8% "not at all motivated") increased to 30 percent (12% "unmotivated," 18% "not at all motivated") in 2020. In one year, that's a 13-percentage-point increase overall in Christians who are unmotivated to address racial injustice, including a doubling of those who say they are "not at all motivated."

How motivated are you to address racial injustice in our society?

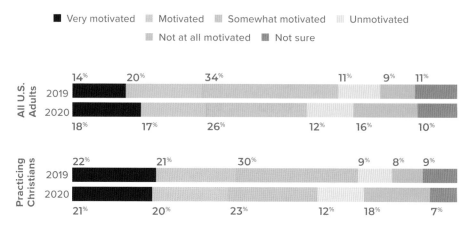

n=2,889 U.S. adults, July 19–August 5, 2019.
n=1,525 U.S. adults, June 18–July 17, 2019.

Looking at the 2019 sample alone, it's clear much of the support for addressing racial injustice originates with practicing Christians of color. White Christians, who are least likely to experience racial injustice, are least motivated to address it (67% white practicing Christians vs. 92% Black, 80% Hispanic, 74% Asian). On this point, white practicing Christians look similar to the general population, with only one-third expressing high motivation.

In the summer 2020 response to this question, there was not a large enough sample of practicing Christians to be broken down by race. But among racial segments in the broader group of self-identified Christians, we see telling patterns—namely, Black Christians are increasingly likely to be "very" motivated, and white Christians are increasingly likely to be "not at all motivated."[35]

What Can One Person Do?

Motivation to act is one thing, a strategy is another. From a list of possible steps individuals could take to improve racial dynamics in the country, building

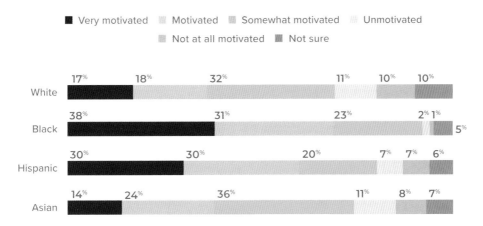

How motivated are you to address racial injustice in our society?

Practicing Christians by race

■ Very motivated   ▨ Motivated   ▨ Somewhat motivated   ▨ Unmotivated
▨ Not at all motivated   ▨ Not sure

White: 17% | 18% | 32% | 11% | 10% | 10%

Black: 38% | 31% | 23% | 2% | 1% | 5%

Hispanic: 30% | 30% | 20% | 7% | 7% | 6%

Asian: 14% | 24% | 36% | 11% | 8% | 7%

n=1,364 practicing Christians, July 19–August 5, 2019.

diverse relationships seems to be the universal response (67% general population, 70% practicing Christians). This option clearly outpaces others as the top choice, regardless of age, race or faith. The nature of this solution matches the perceived nature of the problem: according to most people in the U.S., it's personal, not systemic. But while relationships are an important component of developing empathy and understanding, this research shows it's potentially counterproductive if it's the *only step*.

A broader take on the role of individuals includes efforts to undo unjust systems, perhaps through advocacy, influencing policies or actively seeking a better understanding of race dynamics. Here, differences begin to emerge. In the general population, the second and third most frequently chosen actions were to support the economic thriving of people of color (38%) and to advocate for people of color in leadership positions (33%), a trend that holds across race. In contrast, beyond building diverse relationships, practicing Christians' approach tends toward the evangelistic; half say helping people become Christians is an effective personal means to improve race relations

(47%). This approach is especially favored by white practicing Christians (51%, compared to 40% Black, 36% Hispanic and 41% Asian).

One-third of practicing Christians (34%) emphasizes sharing biblical teachings that encourage special kindness to marginalized groups, a tactic they support as strongly as fostering economic thriving for people of color (34%). Practicing Christians also chose advocacy for leadership opportunities for people of color (26%), though notably less frequently than the general population.

Beyond building diverse relationships, practicing Christians' approach to addressing racial injustice veers toward the evangelistic.

We also discovered, unsurprisingly, evidence of the political polarization around this subject. When it comes to how an individual's vote impacts racial dynamics, these two samples diverge; overall, practicing Christians are more likely to say supporting conservative politicians benefits race relations, while the general population feels the same about supporting liberal politicians. In focus groups, Christians of color often express the pain or sense of betrayal of seeing fellow Christians side with politicians who play to, invoke or even incite racism, both subtle and overt.

Within the Church, strategies for improving racial dynamics strongly differ by race, after the top response of forming cross-cultural friendships. Where white practicing Christians want to lean on faith-sharing, Black practicing Christians want to address minorities' needs for greater economic and leadership opportunity. Overall, all minorities outpace white practicing Christians in their desire to spread a biblical understanding of caring for the vulnerable and marginalized (39% and 32%, respectively).

Let's shift from an intended individual response to a desired institutional response. Specifically, what is the Church's role in improving racial dynamics within our country?

How People Want the Church to Lead on Race

As mentioned in chapter 1, overall, practicing Christians believe churches can help improve race relations by welcoming people of all races into their

How can you, as an individual, improve racial / ethnic dynamics in our country?

All U.S. adults ■ Practicing Christians

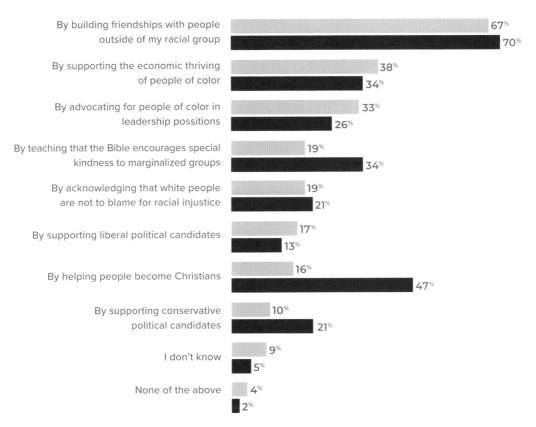

By building friendships with people outside of my racial group
67%
70%

By supporting the economic thriving of people of color
38%
34%

By advocating for people of color in leadership possitions
33%
26%

By teaching that the Bible encourages special kindness to marginalized groups
19%
34%

By acknowledging that white people are not to blame for racial injustice
19%
21%

By supporting liberal political candidates
17%
13%

By helping people become Christians
16%
47%

By supporting conservative political candidates
10%
21%

I don't know
9%
5%

None of the above
4%
2%

n=1,525 U.S. adults, July 19–August 5, 2019.
n=1,364 practicing Christians, July 19–August 5, 2019.

congregations (80%). This remains the top option regardless of respondents' racial category and mirrors the hope of addressing race on an individual level by cultivating more diverse personal circles.

One of the most important positive findings from this study is this: People want the Church to take a place of leadership on these critical topics!

How can you, as an individual, improve racial / ethnic dynamics in our country?
Practicing Christians by race

■ White   ■ Black   ■ Hispanic   ■ Asian

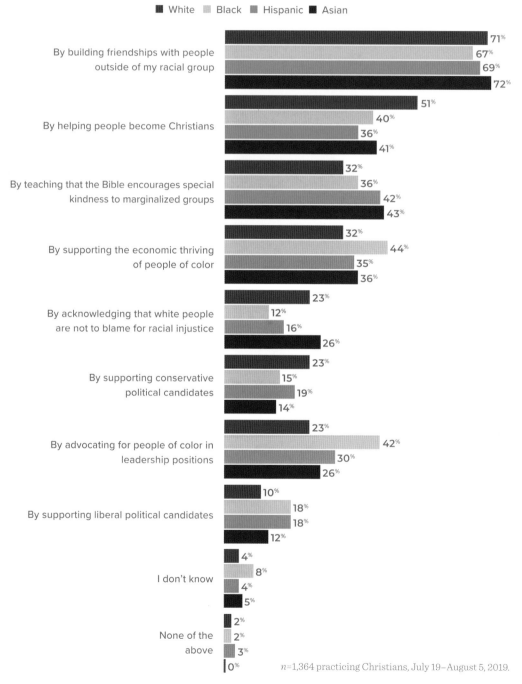

By building friendships with people outside of my racial group
- White: 71%
- Black: 67%
- Hispanic: 69%
- Asian: 72%

By helping people become Christians
- White: 51%
- Black: 40%
- Hispanic: 36%
- Asian: 41%

By teaching that the Bible encourages special kindness to marginalized groups
- White: 32%
- Black: 36%
- Hispanic: 42%
- Asian: 43%

By supporting the economic thriving of people of color
- White: 32%
- Black: 44%
- Hispanic: 35%
- Asian: 36%

By acknowledging that white people are not to blame for racial injustice
- White: 23%
- Black: 12%
- Hispanic: 16%
- Asian: 26%

By supporting conservative political candidates
- White: 23%
- Black: 15%
- Hispanic: 19%
- Asian: 14%

By advocating for people of color in leadership positions
- White: 23%
- Black: 42%
- Hispanic: 30%
- Asian: 26%

By supporting liberal political candidates
- White: 10%
- Black: 18%
- Hispanic: 18%
- Asian: 12%

I don't know
- White: 4%
- Black: 8%
- Hispanic: 4%
- Asian: 5%

None of the above
- White: 2%
- Black: 2%
- Hispanic: 3%
- Asian: 0%

n=1,364 practicing Christians, July 19–August 5, 2019.

How can churches improve race dynamics in our country?

Practicing Christians by race

■ White ■ Black ■ Hispanic ■ Asian

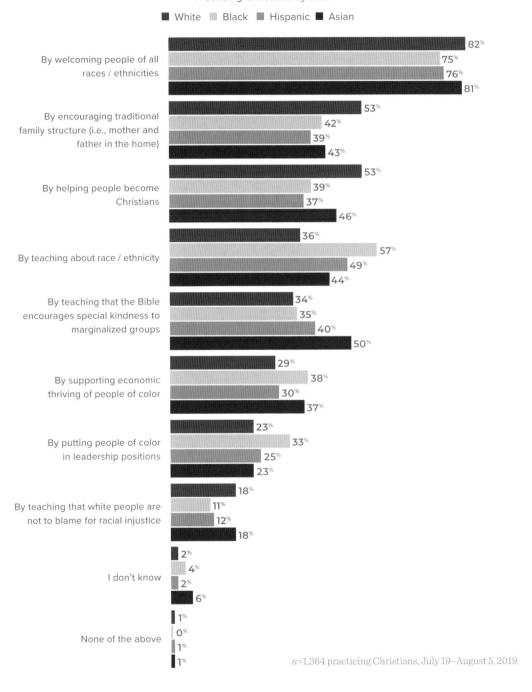

By welcoming people of all races / ethnicities
- 82%
- 75%
- 76%
- 81%

By encouraging traditional family structure (i.e., mother and father in the home)
- 53%
- 42%
- 39%
- 43%

By helping people become Christians
- 53%
- 39%
- 37%
- 46%

By teaching about race / ethnicity
- 36%
- 57%
- 49%
- 44%

By teaching that the Bible encourages special kindness to marginalized groups
- 34%
- 35%
- 40%
- 50%

By supporting economic thriving of people of color
- 29%
- 38%
- 30%
- 37%

By putting people of color in leadership positions
- 23%
- 33%
- 25%
- 23%

By teaching that white people are not to blame for racial injustice
- 18%
- 11%
- 12%
- 18%

I don't know
- 2%
- 4%
- 2%
- 6%

None of the above
- 1%
- 0%
- 1%
- 1%

n=1,364 practicing Christians, July 19–August 5, 2019.

However, beyond forming more diverse congregations, the other ways that practicing Christians want to see the Church help diverge based on the racial group. White practicing Christians favor encouraging traditional family structures (53%); this perhaps reflects their buy-in to the misperception that Black Americans' plight is personal and due to broken family structures (see page 132). The same proportion of white practicing Christians recommends churches improve race dynamics by evangelizing (53%).

- Teaching about race and ethnicity (57%) is important to Black practicing Christians, as well as advocating for more people of color in leadership positions (33%).

- Half of Asians in this Christian segment (50%) say churches should teach from scripture about marginalization, and they join Black peers in pushing for the economic thriving of minorities (37% and 38%, respectively).

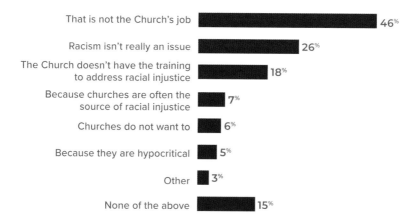

Why do you feel churches should not get involved in improving race relations?

Base: Practicing Christians who believe the Church should not get involved

That is not the Church's job	46%
Racism isn't really an issue	26%
The Church doesn't have the training to address racial injustice	18%
Because churches are often the source of racial injustice	7%
Churches do not want to	6%
Because they are hypocritical	5%
Other	3%
None of the above	15%

n=106 U.S. practicing Christians who do not believe the Church should help improve race relations, July 19–August 5, 2019.

- About one-fifth of white and, interestingly, Asian practicing Christians (18% each) would like churches to clarify that white people are not to blame for racial injustice.

When Christians Stand Back

There is a small minority of practicing Christians (8%) who believe churches cannot or should not help improve race relations in the country. Among them, there is a prevailing sentiment that this is "not the Church's job" (46%); these might be churchgoers who would rather look to other institutions or are unaware of biblical instruction on justice issues. A quarter of this outlying group (26%) posits "racism isn't really an issue." Another one in five (18%), though perhaps likely to see value in addressing injustice, states that the Church does not have the right training.

Others have an actual aversion to the Church's involvement in this area because they feel churches are hypocritical (5%) or the source of the problem to begin with (7%). These may be Christians who bear stories like some of those we heard in focus groups; they have experienced or witnessed racism in the Church firsthand and now find themselves hurting, healing or even leaving the Church.

Who Has the Mic?

As shown earlier in this chapter, one-quarter of practicing Christians says one way churches can help improve race relations in our country is by putting people of color in places of authority. Black practicing Christians in particular see this as an important endeavor.

When a practicing Christian's identity is reflected in the racial composition of the leadership team, they face far fewer hurdles in their worship community.

Both our quantitative and qualitative research suggest that the effort to meaningfully empower people of color to lead the Church bears fruit, but only if leaders of color are in more than token positions. When leaders of color reach critical mass and are given voice, it can help to foster a healthy racial environment in diverse worship communities. When people have a leadership team that looks like them (here, we mean they are part of the same racial group) and has authority to lead or to champion inclusivity in the congregation, it is more likely that they will be integrated into the church body, rather than remaining guests (see page 111).

See the following table: Based on practicing Christians' reports of their own racial identity and the composition of their church's pastoral team, we classified pastoral teams as having the same race as the respondent (Alike) or a different race than the respondent (Unlike). Alternatively, some Christians attend a church where no one racial group is the majority in leadership

Reflecting the Community: Congregants' Experiences by Racial Resemblance with Leadership			
% strongly + somewhat agree	Unlike	Alike	Varied
I find it difficult to move into leadership positions in my church	30%	20%	23%
I find it difficult to build relationships in my church	26%	15%	20%
I feel pressure to give up part of my race / ethnic identity in my church	24%	7%	14%
I have experienced racial prejudice in my church	25%	10%	18%

n=1,364 U.S. practicing Christians, July 19–August 5, 2019.

(Varied). We learn that a practicing Christian in an Unlike leadership context—typically, a churchgoer of color in a white-led church—encounters more significant barriers than in Alike or Varied leadership situations. When a practicing Christian's identity is reflected in the racial composition of the leadership team, they face far fewer hurdles in their worship community.

This data is both a testament to why representation matters and a reminder that a sense of belonging and power-sharing is still rarely extended to leaders or congregants of color in some churches. In focus group research, participants commonly identify barriers to people of color leading in multiracial church environments. Either churches do not have enough leaders of color, or they do not empower them to genuinely impact decisions or provide them with sufficient resources.

Churchgoers of color often express disappointment with the lack of diversity in leadership, noting they feel underrepresented or as if they do not have a voice. Meanwhile, leaders of color in white-led multiracial churches frequently cite significant frustration with lack of support or their church leadership's unwillingness to accept or act upon their input.

Empowering diverse leaders requires more than token representation. It involves a sharing of authority as well as resources. Recommendations from focus group participants advocate for leaders in any context to shift power structures in a way that includes people of color in the right organizational leadership positions where they might actually make a difference and have influence on systems and practices.

Responses to Reparations

One solution to systemic racial injustice proposed by various groups is an effort to redistribute resources historically withheld from Black Americans and make amends for the economic and social impact of the legacy of slavery. There is some precedent for reparations for racial injustices, though these measures have varied in scope and application and have never broadly attempted to correct for the harm inflicted through the slavery era.[36] In 2019, Congress introduced a bill to form a commission to study what reparations for Black Americans could look like. As of this writing, a swell of demonstrations for racial justice have also concentrated on reparations, prompting Southern cities like Asheville, North Carolina to begin taking first steps.[37]

How informed are Christians about reparations? Barna asked practicing Christians how they feel at present about the concept.

White practicing Christians admit having little familiarity with the idea; one-quarter (24%) says they do not know what the term means. For more than one-fifth, however, the word prompts "anger" (22%). In contrast, many Black Christians, feel "hopeful" (33%) and "encouraged" (26%) at the thought of reparations for racial injustice in the U.S. ■

Emotions About "Reparations"

Practicing Christians by race

■ White
▨ Black
▤ Hispanic
■ Asian

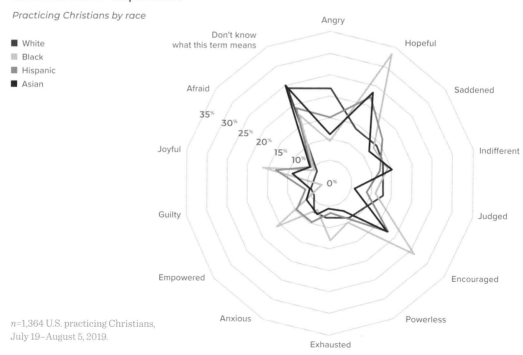

n=1,364 U.S. practicing Christians, July 19–August 5, 2019.

Duke Kwon

CO-AUTHOR OF *REPARATIONS: A CHRISTIAN CALL FOR REPENTANCE AND REPAIR*; LEAD PASTOR OF GRACE MERIDIAN HILL

Reparations of Truth

Reparations is not a new idea. In fact, it has a long and important history in Christian theology and thought. At least as far back as the early 18th century, we find Christians, both Black and white, arguing for restitution to be made for enslaved Africans. I believe Christians today must reclaim reparations as an enduring Judeo-Christian ethic: If you steal something, make amends by giving it back.

But reparations is more than making amends; it's loving our neighbors. Our Black neighbors have been plundered and despoiled by the ravages of white supremacy. As followers of Jesus, we love and serve and give sacrificially, even radically, to those who have been ripped off. This is the ethic of the Good Samaritan, who was not involved in the theft and beating of a man he found lying by the side of the road, but who nonetheless saw it as his moral duty to care for the injured man at great cost to himself. This is Christianity.

It's not only wealth that has been stolen from African Americans, however. There is also the past and ongoing theft of *power* and of *truth*. One of the most egregious forms of theft inflicted upon the Black community by white supremacy is that of the theft of identity. By this I don't mean human beings' fundamental identity as God's image-bearers, which is inviolable and cannot be stolen; rather, I'm referring to the cultural understanding and public narrative of what it means to be Black in America. We have sold lies: an untrue and diminished view of Blackness, the enduring and dehumanizing myths of inherent criminality, romanticized retellings of American history (and American Church history), the erasure of Black history and more.

Restoring the truth means unmasking these lies, repenting of ways we participate in false narratives, memorializing the truth and learning how to tell truer

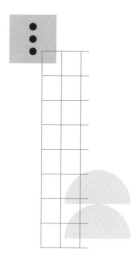

stories about Black identity, dignity and humanity. I believe this is a uniquely Christian calling for this age.

Reparations is more than writing a check—though I do believe that the restoration of plundered wealth must be a part of the work of racial repair. Reparations is a process of restoring the soul of the American Church that begins with truth-telling and repentance of our sinful past. There is no healing that can come about without first telling the truth.

I believe one of the reasons we're so uncomfortable with the idea of reparations is that we have drifted so far from a biblical understanding of restitution. If you steal something, you need to do more than apologize; you have to actually return what you stole. But as individuals—all of us, but most commonly white Christians—we are not persuaded of our culpability. The notion that there is sin for which we must repent is offensive, because we don't have a biblical view of corporate culpability. Culturally speaking, we're deeply committed to radical individualism, and that commitment is a major social and psychological barrier for many evangelicals to understanding and addressing systemic racial injustice. We're on board with personal prejudice and interpersonal brokenness when it comes to race. But an institutional or structural understanding of racial injustice? *No, no! That's Marxist.*

> "We're deeply committed to radical individualism, and that commitment is a major social and psychological barrier for many evangelicals to understanding and addressing systemic racism."

But it's not. It's biblical. This is a failure of teaching, and church leaders must help white Christians—all Christians—recover a biblical framework for collective sin and normalize our language surrounding corporate responsibility.

I think most people resist the idea of righting historic wrongs because they believe something like, "You're imputing the sins of other individuals to me and then punishing me for sins I did not personally commit." But that's not the essential ethic that undergirds a Christian understanding of restitution, which is this: If you inherit something that was stolen long ago, you are in possession of ill-gotten goods. It may have been passed down across many generations, but time does not change the fact that, morally speaking, it doesn't belong to you. There was never a fair and moral transfer of ownership from the person to whom it justly belonged.

Imagine someone knocks on your door one day and says, "I'm sorry to bother you, but the car in your driveway that you've been driving for years, that you believe your mom gave you out of the generosity of her heart, was stolen and is rightfully mine. If you take a look at the title, I think you'll see my name is right there—and I'd appreciate if you gave it back."

You'd naturally want to respond, "This is my car! I've been driving it, paying the insurance premiums and for regular maintenance. Plus, I didn't know my mom stole it!"

But the truth is, it doesn't matter. It doesn't matter that you didn't know. It doesn't matter that you've been taking care of it. It doesn't belong to you. Time has not changed the fact that you're in possession of stolen goods.

We must come to terms with the fact that we are the beneficiaries of theft.

Adapted from an interview with Chad Brennan. Used by permission.

Elena Aronson

DIRECTOR OF TRAINING FOR ARRABON

Discipling Toward Racial Justice

Q. Describe a healthy, godly dynamic between white and Black Christians when it comes to justice and reconciliation.

A. I talk with many Christians who passionately want to see reconciliation between people of all racial and ethnic backgrounds in America. Many are grieved by the prevalence of racially segregated churches and long for greater diversity. I, too, long for a fulfilled vision of Revelation 7:9 where people from every nation, tribe, people and language worship before the throne of God.

However, in our focus on diversity, I think we misdiagnose the problem. If the problem is our separateness, then it is obvious that the solution is togetherness. But any multiethnic church can tell you that getting diverse people in the same room only brings the assurance of conflict, not of kumbaya. Separateness is a *symptom* of a much greater problem, created and maintained over generations, that resides in our economic and legislative systems, impacts our interpersonal relationships and even malforms our spirituality.

Our society, our churches, our relationships and our minds and souls will not be healed from the impact of white supremacy overnight. First off, we need a vision of a transformed society that is informed by the Kingdom so that we can identify what justice and reconciliation truly look like. Then we need to make a plan to get there.

I believe that plan requires different roles because we have all contributed differently to the mess we find ourselves in. Certainly, for a transformed relationship, Black Americans will eventually have to extend grace and forgiveness.

However, insisting on forgiveness without making any movements toward justice and reparation of harm is inappropriate and hurtful. White people need to take ownership of the ways we have contributed to injustice in society, whether through explicit actions or complicit behaviors, and repent. We cannot expect to see a transformed society if we never change our behavior and begin to write a new narrative marked by justice and truth. Black Americans, on the other hand, can keep white Americans accountable by holding us to a standard that is shaped by a vision of the Kingdom, rather than a vision corrupted by privilege. The specifics of that work will look different for each individual, but we cannot ask Black and white Americans to hold the same roles to fix a problem that we had very different roles creating.

Q. Concern for racial justice is stronger among people with greater overall biblical literacy, yet white practicing Christians still lag behind Black and Hispanic Christians when it comes to seeing clear scriptural applications for today's justice issues. What do you make of this gap? How can leaders help white Christians make the connection between discipleship and racial justice?

A. I have certainly witnessed this gap and it does not surprise me. It is one of many ways white supremacy has malformed our spirituality. While people of color in America have had to lament and seek God in the midst of active oppression and injustice, white people have often turned a blind eye. It is very difficult to have a healthy spirituality when you ignore, deny or explain away the suffering of others. In Isaiah 58, the Israelites are performing all kinds of spiritually pious actions and they wonder why God is not answering their prayers. God answers, "Is not this the kind of fasting I have chosen: to loose the chains of injustice and untie the cords of the yoke, to set the oppressed free and break every yoke?" (v. 6). Many white Americans have been discipled to practice personal spiritual piety but were not taught to see justice as an act of worship that is pleasing to God.

"We cannot ask Black and white Americans to hold the same roles to fix a problem that we had very different roles creating."

We desperately need Christian leaders who can reconnect white people's spiritual conversion with racial justice. I think this will require a new type of conversion: a movement from caring about personal moral responsibility to responsibility for those outside your direct social circle and the social, economic and political implications that come as a result. Leaders can help spark these conversions through the messages they preach, the songs they use in worship, the art they create and the way they engage in outreach and missions. We need to learn the practice of lament so that we can bring the brokenness we see in society, and the brokenness in ourselves, before God for transformation. We need to see leaders treat injustice and systemic suffering as pastoral concerns, rather than shying away from anything that might be deemed "political." And we need to expand our practice of confession, remembering how the people of God repeatedly had to confess not only individual but familial, corporate and historic sins in the process of seeking redemption and restoration for their broken communities. ▮

Conclusion from Barna Group

Biblical community.
Authentic diversity.
Reconciliation and justice.
Lives changed.

We aspire to live up to the promise of New Testament faith in our churches and communities. For Christian leaders, what does it truly mean and what will it actually look like to go *beyond diversity*?

For Barna, answering this question practically is not easy, especially given the fact that this has been one of the most difficult projects our team has tackled in nearly four decades of researching the U.S. Church. For starters, it is challenging to report on the findings since there is little agreement on the existence of, vocabulary for, sources of or solutions to racial injustice.

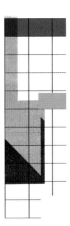

Building a shared vision for what the Church can and should achieve is a critical place to begin. And we firmly believe that solid research is at least a starting place for common ground, a shared understanding of the problems and jointly held ownership for pursuing biblical solutions. No research study is perfect, but at its best, a study such as this can help to translate across perspectives and experiences. It can help us to find and to build upon common ground.

Our research, then, is meant to be not only diagnostic in nature, but also prescriptive in dosing out changed hearts, minds and practices. (The contributions from the experts we convened are more prescriptive, and we encourage you to explore their work beyond these pages.) Some solutions will take years to apply, some are highly unique and local, some won't go far enough on their own. We sincerely hope that our researchers could return to leaders who have been informed or inspired by this data in a few years from now and ask, "What did you do? Why did that work?" Our prayer is that this research sinks in deep and leads you to be a new kind of leader pursuing the transformative work of reconciliation in your church.

For now, here are some next steps that this project—the research, the findings, the experts we've learned from—leads us toward. We believe that pastors and churchgoers of all races in all congregations are meant to be partners in equipping Christians to have a biblical, faithful engagement with matters of racial justice.

This set of conclusions is mostly applicable to white leaders in churches that are either multiracial or aiming to be so. Our findings demand the attention and action of white Christians and urge that diversity has its costs— either because leaders must do the serious, much-needed work of self-examination around ideas of race and justice, or because congregants of color may pay the price if their leaders don't do so. In other words, if you fail to count the cost to lead the Church to a faithful vision of the Body of Christ, someone else will lose.

Our findings demand the attention and action of white Christians and urge that diversity has its costs.

Make no mistake, this study reveals that corners of the Church are woefully ill-equipped and even complicit in ongoing racial prejudice and injustice. A careful, heart-led reading of the data shows that the Christian community in the U.S. has deep problems stemming from racism, white supremacy and racial bias. As researchers called to be eyes and ears of the Church, we do not draw these conclusions lightly or to appear trendy or "woke." As Christians who happen to be proficient at reading the signs of the times, we believe that a failure to accurately describe, sincerely acknowledge and fully repent from the problems we uncover in our research will be a matter of our own faithfulness before the Creator of the universe.

Furthermore, at the center of our work at Barna lies a vision of a well-functioning, mature and resilient Body of Christ—one that demonstrates to the world the power of the gospel. We envision millions of Christians who have not been conformed to the patterns of this world, but whose minds have been transformed by the renewing power of the Word (Romans 12:2).

We imagine a people united with Christ and united together, where the dividing wall of hostility has been broken down (Ephesians 2:13-15). As you consider the implications of this study, nothing less than the public witness of the Church and the faithfulness of our own hearts are at stake.

To Christians and church leaders of color: Your patience and your frustration is seen and acknowledged—even in the data! Your desire to honor and serve God faithfully is carried out alongside white Christians who often don't fully understand—or worse, don't care about—the fallout of the sin of racism. The people behind this project deeply lament the burdens carried by Christians of color and the injustices in our society, our communities and our churches. Our research, interviews and discussions with leaders of color working hard in this space speak to the value of gathering with peers for encouragement and finding time to rest and refresh your soul. We pray for space for you to do this, and to be reminded of how God cherishes you. Thank you for continuing to pursue what is just and what is good.

Form a Foundation of Learning (and Un-learning) About Race

To move beyond diversity, the first recommendation coming from the research is for leaders to be learners. Those leaders who effectively move beyond diversity take intentional efforts to read widely, educate themselves and immerse themselves in the experience of people of color. One great way to do just this is to spend time exploring survey research like this (and other reports from Barna including *Where Do We Go from Here?* and *Trends in the Black Church*). Research can help us to understand the lived experience of other Christians and data has the added benefit of helping leaders to understand the gaps in perception and experience. You might even find that using data to show those gaps to the people you lead would help them to open their eyes to the deeper issues that are easily ignored.

Keep in mind, education is a non-negotiable, but is not sufficient on its own to move fully beyond diversity. The events of 2020 prompted many people to embrace self-education about racism. Yet, despite those efforts, some of the clearest divides in this study still emerge in our most recent polling. Between the summers of 2019 and 2020, gaps in perception of present racial injustice actually grew wider across racial segments— primarily because people with slight resistance or indifference toward

Moving from General Concepts to Practical Help

A NOTE FROM

Dr. Glenn Bracey, Chad Brennan and Dr. Michael O. Emerson

From the beginning of the Race, Religion & Justice Project, our goal has been to provide practical help for the Body of Christ. In order for the information in this book to translate into progress, it will be important for you to answer three important questions:

- How am I doing in these areas?
- How is our organization doing in these areas?
- How can I / we make sustainable progress?

Over the last year, the research team and many experts have invested hundreds of hours developing research-based assessment tools and a coaching network that can help you to answer those essential questions.

For details, visit rjuc.org.

the conversation dug in their heels in denial of a race problem. Acknowledgment especially lags among respondents who are Christian, white and older.

The shift is a reminder that not everybody is in the same book club about racial justice—and only time will tell if interest and education translates to meaningful, tangible action. Even among those whose general awareness and concern is growing, such as younger respondents, specific and systemic manifestations of discrimination aren't always clearly identified. This is what Dr. King called a "shallow understanding from people of good will"—which, to him, was "more frustrating than absolute misunderstanding from people of ill will."[38]

Church leaders and teams can make a long-term, whole-life commitment to improving their understanding of the past and present of race relations. They can also walk with their congregants in identifying how even "good" things—a desire to maintain a place of comfort, for instance—can prevent true repair of injustices. Along the way, they may have to put off the "old self, which is being corrupted by its deceitful desires; to be made new in the attitude of your minds; and to put on the new self, created to be like God in true righteousness and holiness" (Ephesians 4:22–24, NIV).

Being a learning leader requires more than the best curriculum, facilitator or reading list. It requires what all good learning demands: ongoing curiosity, repentance and humility, as well as the godly boldness to speak up, ask questions and gently correct others. For white leaders, it requires being led or even disciplined by leaders of color, which produces humility and highlights different sets of skills and experiences. Having leaders committed to ongoing learning will be crucial for setting the basic conditions for transformation, and these practices can be exercised in both multiracial and monoracial environments.

Seek Sincere (and Not Token) Relationships

A second major recommendation emerging from the research relates to pursuing the right kind of relationships. Sometimes our motivations for seeking greater racial and ethnic representation in a church, or in any group, prioritize superficial or wrong outcomes, such as meeting a quota or maintaining an image. Ultimately, these aims alone risk dehumanizing people of color and using their presence in the service of white individuals or predominantly white organizations.

Christians are called to celebrate and draw near to the image of God in everyone and to seek justice and unity—not just perform diversity.

Broader and better motivations for diverse worship might be to address root causes of racial discrimination or re-examine norms built around the cultural majority. In a deeper spiritual sense, Christians are called to celebrate and draw near to the image of God in everyone and to seek justice and unity—not just perform diversity.

One of the realities to keep in mind is that people of color often bear the brunt of the work when it comes to explaining and exploring issues of reconciliation. If you are in a diverse faith community, what work is being done in your congregation when it comes to education, unity and justice? Who is bearing most of it? Who is benefiting? If you are in a faith community that is more homogeneous, how can you still be learning and working toward racial justice when you don't have as many opportunities for multiracial relationships? Sincere and biblical relationships are a two-way, mutually beneficial partnership.

Consider the Individuals and the Systems

A third recommendation stemming from the research is that Christian leaders (especially white leaders) need to be open and aware of the multi-dimensional nature of racism and racial injustice. Our findings are crystal clear: White Christians tend to think the problems of racism (if they see them at all) are mostly or exclusively due to relational, interpersonal issues; yet, people of color who are Christians (and especially Black believers) tend to perceive the problems to involve both relational *and* institutional issues. Personal and systemic. Demonstrating these huge gaps in perception is, by the way, one of the clearest ways to leverage survey data for the benefit of helping your people's compassion to grow.

Because white Christians have tended to focus—when they do acknowledge the need for reconciliation—on personal, individual and relational problems, the solutions they advance have focused primarily on relationships. That includes ideas such as having friends of other racial groups or joining a multiracial church—efforts that, this study shows, Christians still place high importance on today. In recent decades, there have been good faith efforts toward racial reconciliation, diversity, public apology, repentance and more.

Addressing systemic justice issues, however, has been considered less important, unnecessary or even taboo in the Church at large—even though it is weighed as an important issue among non-white Christians, and some younger Christians. To ignore discrimination that is historically built into our society and institutions is, at minimum, to ignore what congregants of color say are their great concerns and lived experiences. Further, dismissing a systemic context could perpetuate environments where individual relationships are then burdened by inauthenticity, power dynamics and prejudice.

Arrabon founder and *Beyond Diversity* reviewer and contributor David Bailey offers one helpful metaphor to help pastors understand the validity of both types of solutions:

"In America, the law has been established for about 100 years that we have to drive our cars on the right side of the road. If that law were to be reversed immediately today, would our thoughts, attitudes and behaviors change as quickly as the law? How many years do you think it would take before our bias to drive on the right side of the road would change?

"Having people shift from driving from the right side of the road to the left side of the road isn't just a matter of changing people's thoughts, attitudes and actions. There were structures in place to reinforce the thought that driving on the right side of the road is appropriate and normal. Think about all of the systems of traffic lights, signs, road patterns and even vehicle design that would have to be dismantled and new systems that would have to be put into place to support a 'new normal.' Think about how many generations it would take before society was fully rid of the habits and symbols of the old driving system.

"Our country has been organized around (and divided by) race for 350 years, and even as laws and social norms continue to evolve to make racism less acceptable, we have not gone through a transformation in our thoughts, attitudes and actions. We have not finished removing the systems associated with old behaviors and setting up new ones. We have racial biases that we need to be aware of and discipled out of."

As you lead through these micro and macro changes, there will be disorientation along the road, perhaps even collisions. Be prepared, patient and persistent.

Moving Beyond Diversity Is a Discipleship Problem—and Opportunity

Fourth, be encouraged that engaging Christians in racial justice is not a distraction but a powerful means and goal of discipleship. As we learned in our leadership and focus group research, multiracial churches that are functioning well are producing great spiritual and practical fruit. They are seeing lives transformed—including white Christians, who, as Barna has tracked for decades, are at risk of lukewarm faith that is spiritually and culturally inert and causes the loss of emerging generations from the Church.

Engaging Christians in racial justice is not a distraction but a powerful means and goal of discipleship.

Our interviews with church and academic leaders propose that gaps in views of race relations stem in part from theology. By emphasizing personal responsibility to respond to Jesus' gift of salvation and subsequently a personal accountability for spiritual growth and discipleship, many Christians are trained to focus only on "vertical" reconciliation—with God alone. Some church traditions do not emphasize to the same degree the concept of "horizontal" reconciliation—of restoring relationships and systems. The Bible points in both directions. It neither attributes injustice solely to harmful structures nor pins it solely on sinful individuals. Westernized Christianity may place more emphasis on the latter, yet we see heroes of scripture repent for corporate and ancestral sin. We read that "an unplowed field produces food for the poor, but injustice sweeps it away" (Proverbs 13:23, NIV).

Further, a theological orientation that accounts for how the sin of racism has not only infected our hearts but also shaped our systems may actually improve one's ability to embrace more personal, relational solutions to racial tension, emboldening people for honest, empathetic and transformative multiracial community.

We see in our data, sympathize with and pray for the leaders who worry about saying or doing the wrong thing. Addressing topics like these responsibly, compassionately and biblically in a time of profound division is not easy. It means navigating conversations littered with political landmines, polarizing buzzwords and pat answers alike. But even avoiding the hard discussions communicates *something* to your congregants about what it means to be a follower of Christ and a member of your local church. Preaching, teaching and living racial justice is essential to the formation of resilient disciples in our country today, and it is an inescapable part of the sacred burden and calling of modern-day ministry.

You don't have to go it alone. Lean on the scholarship and leadership of other faithful teachers in this space. Study and pray through these issues alongside your team, your peers and your congregants. Ground yourself in scripture, carefully studied in its context and prayerfully applied in yours.

Be Boldly Generous and Sacrificial

Finally, the research recommends that churches consider and correct ways that white normativity holds people of color back in worship and in leadership—even if it means shaking up or letting go of the way things have been. In our focus groups, some stories from white pastors in multiracial churches stood out. These were churches that staffed their teams with both men and women of multiple races and ethnicities. Not only that, these pastors sought input from and deferred to non-white teammates and leaders, even those who were more junior, and even if it meant taking a long time to make decisions. This humility and consideration extended to congregants. Mistakes were still made—but top-down humility paved the way for growth and healthy diversity.

For church leaders, white ones especially, racial justice may mean laying position, status, resources, power and even earned authority at the altar. This can occur whether or not someone is presently in a racially diverse church, neighborhood or city. It might look like donating, giving or redistributing financial resources (personally or as a church) to support racial justice causes or the empowerment of non-white leaders, in your church or others. It might mean white leaders choose to pass the mic to people of color, hire more diversely or decline opportunities where greater racial representation could be needed or beneficial.

Racial justice may mean laying position, status, resources, power and even rightly earned authority at the altar.

These actions don't require perfection, but require time, consistency and, yes, likely inconvenience and sacrifice. After all, "we are looking for the city that is to come. Through Jesus, therefore, let us continually offer to God a sacrifice of praise—the fruit of lips that openly profess his name. And do not forget to do good and to share with others, for with such sacrifices God is pleased" (Hebrews 13:14–16, NIV).

*   *   *

As we have stated, we firmly believe the journey beyond diversity leads toward greater beauty within the Body of Christ, greater unity in churches and also toward the strength and resilience of the Church at large. Imagine a Church that doesn't succumb to cultural shifts which diminish the public credibility and personal practice of Christianity.

Imagine congregants regularly seeking wisdom from God's Word and applying that teaching for the flourishing of their communities. Imagine pastors and churchgoers growing deeper and more committed in their faith, praying, repenting and loving their neighbor as themselves.

Imagine a transformative, merciful, justice-oriented faith that is meaningful and attractive to the next generation and to those outside the Church.

Imagine Christians who take seriously today the charge to "learn to do right, seek justice and defend the oppressed" (Isaiah 1:17, NIV). ▪

Data Tables

Practicing Christians on the Treatment of People of Color & the Treatment of White People

In general, in our country these days, would you say that . . .

■ White ■ Black ■ Hispanic ■ Asian

	In hiring, pay and promotions	When applying for a loan or mortgage	By the courts and justice systems
Black people are treated less fairly than white people	39% / 87% / 62% / 55%	33% / 72% / 53% / 48%	49% / 88% / 68% / 54%
White people are treated less fairly than Black people	14% / 3% / 5% / 8%	7% / 8% / 8% / 6%	7% / 3% / 6% / 5%
Both are treated equally	48% / 10% / 32% / 37%	60% / 19% / 39% / 46%	44% / 8% / 25% / 41%
Hispanic people are treated less fairly than white people	45% / 86% / 65% / 58%	38% / 76% / 56% / 46%	42% / 78% / 64% / 51%
White people are treated less fairly than Hispanic people	12% / 5% / 6% / 8%	9% / 8% / 8% / 11%	8% / 5% / 6% / 8%
Both are treated equally	43% / 9% / 29% / 34%	53% / 16% / 36% / 42%	50% / 18% / 30% / 41%
Asian / Asian American people are treated less fairly than white people	20% / 56% / 38% / 44%	14% / 44% / 25% / 24%	16% / 49% / 24% / 32%
White people are treated less fairly than Asian / Asian American people	8% / 8% / 14% / 5%	9% / 14% / 22% / 4%	7% / 13% / 15% / 4%
Both are treated equally	72% / 36% / 48% / 51%	77% / 42% / 54% / 72%	77% / 38% / 61% / 64%

n=1,364 practicing Christians, July 19–August 5, 2019.
n=624 Hispanic and Asian practicing Christians, May 22–June 5, 2020.

Practicing Christians on Reasons for Inequity

Based on statistics, on average BLACK people have lower quality jobs, housing and income than white people. Why do you think this is?

Aggregate of all selected statements

	WHITE	BLACK	HISPANIC	ASIAN
Because many Black people experience ongoing discrimination	30%	69%	49%	42%
Because many Black people were discriminated against in the past	29%	48%	45%	41%
Because there were laws that favored white people in the past	17%	38%	31%	23%
Because people do not trust that Black people will make good leaders	12%	31%	25%	16%
Because many Black people lack educational opportunities	37%	25%	33%	44%
Because many white people get help from their families / personal connections	14%	24%	15%	13%
Because many Black fathers leave their families	33%	12%	13%	18%
Because many Black people rely on government assistance	26%	11%	16%	25%
Because Black culture discourages them from success	20%	11%	17%	13%
Because many Black people have less natural ability	3%	8%	3%	7%
Because of language barriers	5%	4%	5%	4%
Because many white people work harder	9%	3%	6%	9%
Because God favors white people	1%	3%	3%	2%
I don't believe it is true that Black people have lower quality jobs, housing and income	21%	5%	13%	14%

n=1,364 practicing Christians, July 19–August 5, 2019.
n=624 Hispanic and Asian practicing Christians, May 22–June 5, 2020..

Practicing Christians on Reasons for Inequity

Based on statistics, on average **HISPANIC** *people have lower quality jobs, housing and income than white people. Why do you think this is?*

Aggregate of all selected statements

	WHITE	BLACK	HISPANIC	ASIAN
Because many Hispanic people experience ongoing discrimination	30%	49%	46%	34%
Because of language barriers	46%	48%	43%	47%
Because many Hispanic people lack educational opportunities	41%	26%	39%	48%
Because many Hispanic people were discriminated against in the past	24%	40%	34%	30%
Because people do not trust that Hispanic people will make good leaders	15%	23%	23%	12%
Because many white people get help from their families / personal connections	14%	17%	15%	15%
Because many Hispanic people rely on government assistance	22%	10%	11%	23%
Because Hispanic culture discourages them from success	13%	12%	10%	11%
Because many Hispanic fathers leave their families	8%	4%	6%	6%
Because many Hispanic people have less natural ability	3%	7%	7%	9%
Because there were laws that favored white people in the past	4%	11%	5%	12%
Because many white people work harder	6%	6%	3%	7%
Because God favors white people	3%	2%	3%	5%
I don't believe it is true that Hispanic people have lower quality jobs, housing and income	22%	8%	14%	13%

n=1,364 practicing Christians, July 19–August 5, 2019.

n=624 Hispanic and Asian practicing Christians, May 22–June 5, 2020.

Practicing Christians on Reasons for Inequity

*Based on statistics, on average, **ASIAN** people are less likely to be promoted into management positions. Why do you believe this is??*

Aggregate of all selected statements

	WHITE	BLACK	HISPANIC	ASIAN
Because many Asian people experience ongoing discrimination	27%	46%	29%	41%
Because of language barriers	30%	34%	22%	33%
Because many Asian people were discriminated against in the past	24%	32%	23%	30%
Because people do not trust that Asian people will make good leaders	16%	28%	11%	30%
Because there were laws that favored white people in the past	11%	35%	20%	19%
Because many white people get help from their families / personal connections	8%	22%	14%	17%
Because many Asian people lack educational opportunities	7%	7%	13%	10%
Because Asian culture discourages them from success	5%	12%	11%	6%
Because many Asian people have less natural ability	4%	5%	8%	5%
Because many white people work harder	4%	5%	8%	5%
Because many Asian people rely on government assistance	4%	7%	8%	3%
Because many Asian fathers leave their families	3%	4%	7%	5%
Because God favors white people	3%	1%	7%	1%
I don't believe it is true that Asian people are less likely than white people to be promoted into management positions	51%	21%	40%	32%

n=1,364 practicing Christians, July 19–August 5, 2019.
n=624 Hispanic and Asian practicing Christians, May 22–June 5, 2020.

Practicing Christians on the Advantage or Disadvantage of Their Race

Overall, has the following helped or hurt your ability to get ahead?

■ Helped a lot ▦ Helped a little ▦ Neither helped nor hurt

▦ Hurt a little ▦ Hurt a lot ■ No answer

	Helped a lot	Helped a little	Neither helped nor hurt	Hurt a little	Hurt a lot	No answer
Being white	17%	20%	55%	3%	2%	3%
Being Black	16%	8%	36%	23%	14%	3%
Being Hispanic	19%	13%	38%	24%	4%	1%
Being Asian	11%	12%	51%	16%	5%	5%

n=1,364 practicing Christians, July 19–August 5, 2019.
n=624 Hispanic and Asian practicing Christians, May 22–June 5, 2020.

Methodology

This multi-faceted research study involved multiple phases of data collection in 2019 and 2020.

Qualitative research: Focus group interviews were conducted with 200 individuals from 20 churches and five cities. Group types covered men and women and multiple races, with the goal of examining the extensive diversity of peoples. Additional leader interviews were conducted with 67 leaders and experts and 68 church staff members from three churches.

Quantitative research: This study of 2,889 U.S. adults was conducted online between July 19 and August 5, 2019, via a national consumer panel. The survey over-sampled practicing Christians and Black, Asian and Hispanic adults. Statistical weighting has been applied in order to maximize representation by age, gender, ethnicity, education and region. The margin of error is plus or minus 1.9 points at a 95 percent confidence interval.

In 2020, Barna (in partnership with Dynata) repeated some questions in a survey of 1,525 U.S. adults conducted online between June 18 and July 6, 2020, via a national consumer panel. The survey over-sampled Black, Asian and Hispanic adults. Statistical weighting has been applied in order to maximize representation by age, gender, ethnicity, education and region. The margin of error is plus or minus 1.8 points at a 95 percent confidence interval.

Acknowledgments

The researchers are tremendously grateful to the Lilly Endowment for their support, financial and otherwise, of this study.

Several contributors generously shared from their experience and expertise and strengthened this report: Elena Aronson, Eliezer Bonilla, Jr., Raymond Chang, Dominique DuBois Gilliard, Duke Kwon, Alexia Salvatierra and Dorena Williamson.

With direction from Joe Jensen and OX Creative, Ricky Linn created the cover design. The research and writing team included: Dr. Glenn Bracey, Chad Brennan, Daniel Copeland, Dr. Michael O. Emerson, Brooke Hempell and Brittany Wade. Alyce Youngblood edited the report. David Bailey and Oneya Okuwobi reviewed the manuscript and offered crucial feedback and recommendations for application. Joan Chen-Main and Verónica Thames contributed to writing and editorial assistance, and Doug Brown proofread the report. Annette Allen designed infographics and internal design standards, and Rob Williams completed internal layout. Brenda Usery managed production with project management assistance from Elissa Clouse. The project team thanks our Barna colleagues Amy Brands, Jeni Cohen, Aidan Dunn, Kristin Jackson, Pam Jacob, Savannah Kimberlin, David Kinnaman, Steve McBeth, Matt Randerson, Traci Stark and Todd White.

Many thanks to the RJUC Collaboration Team, who played a vital role in this study. This report would not exist without their input on the direction, topics and surveys and their help in connecting people to participate in the research. A special thank you to the 68 members who took the time to provide us valuable feedback on our study design and questions. Thanks also to the interview respondents and focus group participants. We are not including their names to maintain anonymity.

About the Project Partners

Barna Group is a research firm dedicated to providing actionable insights on faith and culture, with a particular focus on the Christian Church. In its 35-year history, Barna has conducted more than two million interviews in the course of hundreds of studies and has become a go-to source for organizations that want to better understand a complex and changing world from a faith perspective. Barna's clients and partners include a broad range of academic institutions, churches, non-profits and businesses.

barna.com

The Racial Justice and Unity Center is a new ministry of **Renew Partnerships**. Renew Partnerships is a non-profit Christian organization focused on helping Christian individuals and organizations work toward biblical racial justice and unity. Renew provides training and assessment resources which are based on biblical principles, national research and the input of leading experts. In its 15-year history, Renew has worked with thousands of leaders and hundreds of organizations including churches, Christian colleges, seminaries, K–12 schools and campus ministries.

renewpartnerships.org
rjuc.org

Research Sponsor
Lilly Endowment Inc. is a private philanthropic foundation based in Indianapolis. The endowment supports the causes of community, development, education and religion, with special emphasis on projects that benefit young people and that strengthen financial self-sufficiency in the charitable sector. They fund significant programs throughout the United States.

lillyendowment.org

Endnotes

1   Edwards, Korie Little, "The Multiethnic Church Movement Hasn't Lived up to Its
    Promise," *Christianity Today*, https://www.christianitytoday.com/ct/2021/march/
    race-diversity-multiethnic-church-movement-promise.html. In this reference, evangeli-
    cal Protestants are defined by having made a personal commitment to Jesus Christ that is
    important to them and by their belief in: the Bible's accuracy, a responsibility to share
    religious beliefs, eternity in heaven through Jesus Christ and not good works, and Jesus
    having lived a sinless life. This definition of evangelical varies somewhat from Barna's
    legacy evangelical segment.

2   Barna Group, "What's on the Minds of America's Pastors," February 20,2020, https://www.
    barna.com /research/whats_on_mind_americas_pastors/.

3   Barna Group, "Barna's Race Today Briefing," 2020.

4   Barna Group, "Interview – Tim Keller: State of the Church 2020 Webcast," https://vimeo.
    com/420910978.

5   Barna Group, *Gen Z* [Vol. 1] (Ventura, CA: Barna, 2018); Barna Group, "U.S. Adults Have
    Few Friends—and They're Mostly Alike," October 23, 2018, https://www.barna.com/
    research/friends-loneliness/; Barna Group, *Where Do We Go from Here?* (Ventura, CA:
    Barna, 2019); Barna Group, "Americans Soften on Immigration in 2017," September 19,
    2017, https://www.barna.com/research/americans-soften-immigration-2017/.

6   Okuwobi, Oneya Fennell. "'Everything that I've Done Has Always Been Multiethnic':
    Biographical Work among Leaders of Multiracial Churches," *Sociology of Religion* 80, no. 4
    (2019): 478–495.

7   Barna Group, *The State of Pastors* (Ventura, CA: Barna, 2017).

8   Kinnaman, David, "Barna's Perspective on Race and the Church," June 17, 2020, https://
    www.barna.com /barnas-perspective-on-race-and-the-church/.

9   A previous statistical standard for multiracial churches, as defined by Dr. Michael
    Emerson and Christian Smith in their book *Divided by Faith*, was a congregation where no
    single ethnic group comprised more than 80 percent of the congregation. The 2019 study
    only has respondents' estimates of congregational diversity, not actual data on congrega-
    tions, and respondents may greatly overestimate diversity. A 60-percent threshold based
    on respondents' estimates of diversity operates similar to an 80-percent threshold when
    actual congregational diversity data is used.

10   Learn more at https://www.dictionary.com/e/race-vs-ethnicity/; https://www.national-geographic.com /culture/topics/reference/race-ethnicity/; Harper, Lisa Sharon, *The Very Good Gospel* (Colorado Springs, CO: Waterbrook, 2016) Ch. 9.

11   Bracey, Glenn E. and Wendy Leo Moore, "'Race Tests': Racial Boundary Maintenance in White Evangelical Churches," *Sociological Inquiry* 87, Issue 2.

12   Pew Research Center, "The countries with the 10 largest Christian populations and the 10 largest Muslim populations," April 1, 2019, https://www.pewresearch.org/fact-tank/2019/04/01/the-countries-with-the-10-largest-christian-populations-and-the-10-largest-muslim-populations/; Pew Research Center, "Global Christianity—A Report on the Size and Distribution of the World's Christian Population," December 19, 2011, https://www.pewforum.org/2011/12/19/global-christianity-exec/.

13   Barna, *Gen Z* [Vol.1]; Barna Group, *The Connected Generation* (Ventura, CA: Barna, 2019).

14   Dougherty, Kevin D., Mark Chaves, and Michael O. Emerson. 2020. "Racial Diversity in U.S. Congregations, 1998-2019." *Journal for the Scientific Study of Religion* 59(4): 651–662.

15   Bird, Warren and Scott Thumma, "Megachurch 2020: The Changing Reality in America's Largest Churches," https://faithcommunitiestoday.org/wp-content/uploads/2020/10/Megachurch-Survey-Report_HIRR_FACT-2020.pdf.

16   Buchanan, Larry, Quoctrung Bui and Jugal K. Patel, "Black Lives Matter May Be the Largest Movement in U.S. History," *The New York Times*, July 3, 2020, https://www.nytimes.com/interactive/2020/07/03/us /george-floyd-protests-crowd-size.html.

17   Pew Research Center, "Recent protest attendees are more racially and ethnically diverse, younger than Americans overall," June 24, 2020, https://www.pewresearch.org/fact-tank/2020/06/24/recent-protest-attendees-are-more-racially-and-ethnically-diverse-younger-than-americans-overall/.

18   Emerson, Michael O., and Christian Smith, *Divided by Faith: Evangelical Religion and the Problem of Race in America* (Oxford: Oxford University Press, 2000), pp 76.

19   Smith, Candis Watts and Christopher DeSante, "The Racial Views of White Americans—Including Millennials—Depend on the Questions Asked," January 12, 2018, Scholars Strategy Network, https://scholars.org/contribution/racial-views-white-americans-including-millennials-depend-questions-asked.

20   Hannah-Jones, Nikole, "What Is Owed," *The New York Times Magazine*, June 30, 2020, https://www.nytimes .com/interactive/2020/06/24/magazine/reparations-slavery.html; Kraus, Michael W. *et al.*, "The Misperception of Racial Economic Inequality," *Perspectives on Psychological Science* 14:6 (September 10,2019) https://journals.sagepub.com/doi/full/10.1177/1745691619863049.

21   USA Facts, "Black Americans make up 13% of the US population. They Make up 23% of COVID-19 deaths," June 18, 2020, https://usafacts.org/articles/covid-deaths-race-state-age-black-hispanic-white/.

22   Board of Governors of the Federal Reserve System, "Disparities in Wealth by Race and Ethnicity in the 2019 Survey of Consumer Finances," September 28, 2020, https://www.federalreserve.gov/econres/notes/feds-notes/disparities-in-wealth-by-race-and-ethnici-

ty-in-the-2019-survey-of-consumer-finances-20200928.htm; USA Facts, "White people own 86% of wealth and make up 60% of the population," June 25, 2020, https://usafacts. org/articles/white-people-own-86-wealth-despite-making-60-population/; Pew Research Center, "Racial, gender wage gaps persist in U.S., despite some progress," July 1, 2016, https://www .pewresearch.org/fact-tank/2016/07/01/racial-gender-wage-gaps-per-sist-in-u-s-despite-some-progress/; USA Facts, "Percent of people in poverty," https:// usafacts.org/data/topics/people-society/poverty/poverty-measures/poverty-rate-of-all-persons/; USA Facts, "Percent of families in poverty," https://usafacts.org/data /topics/ people-society/poverty/poverty-measures/poverty-rate-of-all-families/; Van C. Tran, Jennifer Lee and Tiffany J. Huang Revisiting the Asian second-generation advantage, Ethnic and Racial Studies 42:13, 2248–2269, DOI: 10.1080/01419870.2019.1579920.

23   USA Facts, "How uneven educational outcomes begin, and persist, in the US," September 4, 2020, https://usafacts.org/articles/educational-attainment-outcome-gaps/.

24   USA Facts, "Homeownership rates show that Black Americans are currently the least likely group to own homes," July 28,2020, https://usafacts.org/articles/homeowner-ship-rates-by-race/; USA Facts, "People in subsidized public housing," https://usafacts. org/data/topics/people-society/poverty/public-housing /people-in-subsidized-housing/; U.S. Department of Housing and Urban Development, Office of Policy Development and Research, "Assisted Housing: National and Local," dataset, https://www.huduser.gov / portal/datasets/assthsg.html#2009-2019_data.

25   The Sentencing Project, "Criminal Justice Facts," https://www.sentencingproject.org/ criminal-justice-facts/; The Sentencing Project, "Report to the United Nations on Racial Disparities in the U.S. Criminal Justice System," April 19, 2018, https://www.sentencing-project.org/publications/un-report-on-racial-disparities/; USA Facts, "Prisoners," https:// usafacts.org/data/topics/security-safety/crime-and-justice/jail-and-prisons/prisoners/; Ava Duvernay, *13th*, Netflix, 2016.

26   Sreenivasan, Hari, Sam Weber and Connie Kargbo, "The true story behind the 'welfare queen' stereotype," June 1, 2019, https://www.pbs.org/newshour/show/the-true-story-behind-the-welfare-queen-stereotype; Lopez, German, "Debunking the most pervasive myth about black fatherhood," https://www.vox.com/2015/6/21/8820537/black-fathers-day; Richardson, Saeed, "Breaking myths about black fatherhood this Father's Day," June 13, 2019, https:// www.chicagoreporter.com/breaking-myths-about-black-fatherhood-this-fathers-day/.

27   Gerdeman, Dina, "Minorities who 'Whiten' Job Resumes Get More Interviews," May 17, 2017, Harvard Business School, https://hbswk.hbs.edu/item/minorities-who-whiten-job-resumes-get-more-interviews.

28   Katznelson, Ira, *When Affirmative Action Was White* (New York: Norton, 2005).

29   act.tv, "Systemic Racism Explained," April 16, 2019, YouTube, https://www.youtube.com/ watch?v=YrHIQIO_bdQ; Vischer, Phil, "Holy Post - Race in America," YouTube, June 14, 2020, https://www.youtube.com/watch?v=AGUwcs9qJXY.

30   Edwards, Korie, *The Elusive Dream: The Power of Race in Interracial Churches* (Oxford: Oxford University Press, 2008).

31   Hill, Daniel, *White Lies: Nine Ways to Expose and Resist the Racial Systems that Divide Us*, (Grand Rapids, MI: Zondervan, 2020).

32   Budiman, Abby, Pew Research Center, "Key findings about U.S. immigrants," August 20,2020, https://www .pewresearch.org/fact-tank/2019/06/17/key-findings-about-u-s-immigrants/.

33   Amos, Deborah, "Biden Plan to Reopen America to Refugees After Trump Slashed Admissions," NPR News, November 11, 2020, https://www.npr.org/2020/11/11/933500132/biden-plans-to-reopen-america-to-refugees-after-trump-slashed-admissions.

34   Barna, "Race Today Briefing," 2020.

35   Barna, "Race Today Briefing," 2020.

36   Hassan, Adeel and Jack Healy, "America Has Tried Reparations Before. Here Is How It Went," *The New York Times*, June 19, 2019, https://www.nytimes.com/2019/06/19/us/reparations-slavery.html.

37   Vigdor, Neil, "North Carolina City Approves Reparations for Black Residents," *The New York Times*, July 16, 2020, https://www.nytimes.com/2020/07/16/us/reparations-asheville-nc.html

38   King, Martin Luther, Jr., *Letter from the Birmingham Jail* (San Francisco: Harper San Francisco, 1994).